D0729842

WHY NOT ME?!?

12 LESSONS A YEAR ON AN ISLAND TAUGHT ME ABOUT LIVING MY DREAMS, AND HOW YOU CAN LIVE YOURS TOO

STACY HOPE SMALL

BALBOA.
PRESS

A DIVISION OF HAY HOUSE

Copyright © 2019 Stacy Hope Small.

All rights reserved. No part of this book may be used or reproduced by any means, graphic, electronic, or mechanical, including photocopying, recording, taping or by any information storage retrieval system without the written permission of the author except in the case of brief quotations embodied in critical articles and reviews.

Balboa Press books may be ordered through booksellers or by contacting:

Balboa Press
A Division of Hay House
1663 Liberty Drive
Bloomington, IN 47403
www.balboapress.com
1 (877) 407-4847

Because of the dynamic nature of the Internet, any web addresses or links contained in this book may have changed since publication and may no longer be valid. The views expressed in this work are solely those of the author and do not necessarily reflect the views of the publisher, and the publisher hereby disclaims any responsibility for them.

The author of this book does not dispense medical advice or prescribe the use of any technique as a form of treatment for physical, emotional, or medical problems without the advice of a physician, either directly or indirectly. The intent of the author is only to offer information of a general nature to help you in your quest for emotional and spiritual well-being. In the event you use any of the information in this book for yourself, which is your constitutional right, the author and the publisher assume no responsibility for your actions.

Any people depicted in stock imagery provided by Getty Images are models, and such images are being used for illustrative purposes only.
Certain stock imagery © Getty Images.

Print information available on the last page.

ISBN: 978-1-9822-2170-6 (sc)
ISBN: 978-1-9822-2172-0 (hc)
ISBN: 978-1-9822-2171-3 (e)

Library of Congress Control Number: 2019901537

Balboa Press rev. date: 02/14/2019

DEDICATION

This book is dedicated to Jerry & Sheila Small, my parents/angels. I have no doubt they are reading it from above.

CONTENTS

Acknowledgments ix

Foreword xiii

Introduction xvii

Lesson 1: You Can't Stop the Waves but You Can Learn to Surf....1

Lesson 2: Anything is Possible When You Believe 7

Lesson 3: Peace is the Word.. 16

Lesson 4: The Bigger the Storm, the Brighter the Rainbow 24

Lesson 5: Your Family is the Ohana You Choose.........................29

Lesson 6: Dogs, Not Diamonds, are a Girl's Best Friend 36

Lesson 7: Fences (and Goats) Make for Great Neighbors............ 46

Lesson 8: Island Time is the Right Time, Trust the (Slow)
           Process... 51

Lesson 9: No One Cares What You Do or What You Drive 58

Lesson 10: Choosing JOY is Always an Option 66

Lesson 11: Health is True Wealth and Self-Care is NOT Selfish...73

Lesson 12: Live Pono, Have Hope, Keep the Faith and
           Practice Aloha... 81

ACKNOWLEDGMENTS

During my extended time on Maui, I learned one of the most important words—other than ALOHA—is *MAHALO.* It is the Hawaiian word for "Thank You" and so much more. Mahalo translates to authentic gratitude, and that means everything to a culture that thrives on graciousness. I have a long list of people I am so very grateful to, for all they taught me, and for all they helped me with during my darkest days. Some of them I met on Maui, some I have known for this entire lifetime, still there are others I am sure I have known in many lifetimes.

For starters, a big huge MAHALO to two of my closest friends—*Beth Villa Hurwitz* and *Alyson Nash*—who are truly part of the OHANA I have chosen to call my family for decades. These are the soul sister/friends who have been there with me as I survived both parents' funerals; on the receiving end of the calls when I've been heartbroken as well as to celebrate joyful times and success. These are the types of friends who will always be my friends, simply because life wouldn't be bearable without either of them.

To my real life sister, *Marcy*, thank you for teaching me the meaning of compassion (from a distance) and nonjudgment. I love you.

To *Wendy Burk*, who I sometimes politely refer to as my "Work Mom" because I (and my company) really needed and still need one, but who has become such an important friend, another member of my chosen OHANA. I couldn't get through a day without the support you and your Cadence Travel team bring to me and my Elite Travel team.

To my editor, *Stephanie Elliot*. So grateful to you! Thank you for sitting with me on the phone going over this manuscript line-by-line to make sure we spelled every singer's name correctly and didn't miss a run-on sentence! Thank you to *Irene Zutell* for introducing us!

To my coach/friend/mentor *Nancy Levin*, who has kicked my ass every time I needed to make major life changes—be it giving back the engagement ring that didn't belong on my finger to getting this book written chapter by chapter to tuning into my intuition and setting boundaries and staying true to my truth. I love you SO much for being you and for inspiring me to be the best version of me.

I am so grateful to those of you I was fortunate to be led to on Maui, as you all collectively helped me heal and discover who I really am. These gifted beautiful souls include: *Lucia Maya, Deborah Manzano, Naya Rice, Hoku on Maui, Jules Harris, Dr. Gina Kim, Dr. Bonnie Marsh* and *Natalie Young*. And, to the most amazing chef who said yes to the challenge of creating the healthy, healing, grain-free meals Dr. Bonnie prescribed for me, thank you *Chef Nicole Scharer*. I love you for flying to San Diego for my 49th birthday BBQ/housewarming party. You are one of a kind.

To my incredible fascinating clients, many who have become friends and confidantes over the years. Thank you for trusting me with your most valuable asset—your time—and allowing me to create life-changing travel experiences for you, whether from my home office in

California or while I was on Maui. Your patience during my reboot and your never-ending trust in me means everything, and you all inspire me to keep changing the world through travel experiences of a lifetime.

To my incredible team at *Elite Travel International*, you all are very special to me as you represent to the world the brand I had no idea I was setting out to build in 2005. Well, maybe I had a clue that I wanted to build a different kind of luxury travel firm, but I couldn't have envisioned a better team of colleagues to join me on the journey to where we are today. Here's to decades more of fun and changing lives #ETISTYLE.

To someone very special to me, whose presence on my journey is still a work-in-progress. Thank you for showing up and for the lessons you've brought to me, even though I've not always understood them at the time. Your role in my life continues to teach me patience, hope, faith, unconditional love & the never-ending amount of trust in the Law of Divine Timing. You inspire me by continuing to force me to shine my light internally and externally, and to show up as the best possible version of myself while inspiring you and hopefully, others to do the same.

Thank you to anyone in this world who rescues dogs who need forever homes. As a serial dog rescuer, I love you all. I can't save all of the dogs, so thank you to those who help the dogs who need a safe home and a place to give and receive their unconditional love. Thank you Lhasa Happy Homes, San Diego Spaniel Rescue, Pet Orphans Fund, LA Love & Leashes and the Palm Beach Humane Society for protecting the pups meant for me until we found each other in this lifetime.

To the doctors and coaches and therapists and healers and yoga teachers and meditation guides and bodyworkers and energy healers and mediums and everyone else I've encountered along my life path/ healing journey: THANK YOU. It takes a village. I am grateful to

ALL of you (including *Dr. Kathleen Mojas, Reeca Gaspari, Dr. Amy Chadwick, Dr. Ryan Gessay, Scott Olsen, Rebecca Rosen, Sarah Renee, Suze Yalof Schwartz, Mallika Chopra, Deepak Chopra, Gabby Bernstein, Diana Seuffert, Dr. Shiva Lalezar*). MAHALO a million times for your role in my world.

And, one last Mahalo to my spiritual musical hero, *Michael Franti*. Your music remains the theme of my life since I first saw you perform as John Mayer's opening act at Madison Square Garden a decade ago. Your authentic lyrics and incredibly upbeat songs inspire me nearly every day. The song STILL STANDING sums it all up. That was my chosen theme for this book long before you pulled me out of the crowd and danced with me and sang *11:59* to me minutes before we moved into 2019. You and your beautiful wife Sarah Franti, your band, Victoria Canal and everyone else who was part of the New Year's Eve concert at Belly Up in Solana Beach not only rocked my world, but gave love and light and huge doses of JOY to everyone in the crowd. The world needs more SOULROCKERS like you. MAHALO.

FOREWORD

Is there something you really, really want to do, or have, but consistently talk yourself out of because it's "unrealistic?" Do you keep yourself so overscheduled and busy, even when you desperately need a break, because slowing down would mean you're lazy, irresponsible and lack value? Are you fed up with watching other people lead happy, peaceful and fulfilling lives while either wondering when it'll be your turn, or just believing it's not meant for you?

If any of these sound familiar, then it's time to ask yourself: "WHY NOT ME?!?"

For much of my life, I thought fun was for other people. As an overachiever and people-pleaser who never wanted to rock the boat, I was constantly seeking external validation and approval. I put everyone else's wants, dreams and needs before mine and prided myself in how much I could *do*, believing that would determine my worth. I spent my days managing the perceptions of others, projecting an image of perfection. In the process, I forgot something.

I forgot to live my own life. And that's no way to live.

This book you are holding is an invitation to your fully inhabited life, a map to the treasure of aliveness within you.

I've had the honor of coaching Stacy since July 2017 and have witnessed her tremendous transformation firsthand. In fact, her journey so powerfully and perfectly embodies what I call my Transformation Equation: Change = Vision + Choice + Action.

Even with her roots in the power of faith and manifestation, Stacy's commitment to her own evolution is palpable, and contagious. I've cherished the opportunity to hold her accountable to taking action in the direction of her desires.

Having coached thousands of people to embrace fear and welcome change through truth-telling, whether it be relationship transitions, switching careers, geographical relocations and setting boundaries, to name a few, I've also made my own jumps that include a contentious divorce after a long-term marriage and quitting my prestigious position as Event Director at Hay House, Inc. to lead an entrepreneurial life as a coach, author and speaker, and I've seen that no matter what the external jump is, the internal jump is always a deepening of self-awareness, self-acceptance, self-compassion, self-forgiveness, self-love and self-worth.

As I've written about in my books *Jump … And Your Life Will Appear, Worthy: Boost Your Self-Worth to Grow Your Net Worth,* and *The New Relationship Blueprint,* it's high time we stop packaging ourselves to be digestible to others. We need to find our no to free our yes and put ourselves first instead! Take a risk, do it different, show up revealed and in truth.

My wish for you is that you'll let this book be a beacon, illuminating the path of what's possible (everything!) And that Stacy's story will support you in dissolving the limits around what you allow yourself to receive, while reminding you that love is an inside job, joy is a choice and peace is a place within.

Nancy Levin
Salida, Colorado
February 2019

INTRODUCTION

Like many of you probably have, I've sought advice from self-help books on how to find peace, choose joy and love life after serious loss. So why share my story? We all have stories. I get that. But, we don't all confront the raw truth and take action to course correct when our life veers off path. I did. *Why Not Me?!?* aims to share not just what I learned from other inspirational authors like Gabrielle Bernstein, Mallika Chopra, Nancy Levin and Louise Hay, but to inspire you by allowing my own fears, grief, resilience and faith in the higher power to shine light on the truth, which is: ***If I can do it, so can you.*** Not convinced? Read on.

If anyone had told me a decade ago that by 2018 I'd be running an eight-figure luxury travel business from an office in my oceanfront dream home and driving a Porsche, I'd have laughed. It seriously wasn't that long ago that I could barely even pay my rent. My dad got cancer and died at 63 leaving me in a traumatized state of depression that I couldn't shake. At the same time, my 60-year-old mom was battling stage 4 metastatic breast cancer. My own health was spiraling downward, as I found myself battling anemia and mono while at the same time recovering from a toxic relationship, and struggling to find new travel clients.

Quick refresher: This was the post-Madoff era, swine flu and worldwide safety concerns were a reality, the economy sucked, and high-end travel had taken a serious hit. We were all struggling to keep our businesses alive, but I intuitively knew all would somehow be okay. I wasn't going to panic, but I was getting ready to put my college waitressing skills to use if needed. Thankfully, I didn't have to moonlight to make rent, but it didn't just "happen" that my business turned around and soon, a rush of new clients and plenty of revenue flowed my way.

In 2010, four years after my dad died, I was still feeling lost. I am not sure why, other than knowing intuitively to follow my inner-GPS, I began to look up at night and pray to whoever was listening to guide me down the right path. It felt like the right (and only) option to help me bust out of being stuck, professionally and personally.

I hadn't yet had my full-on spiritual awakening (that happened the day my mom died in 2014), but the book sitting on my night table was called *The Joys of Much Too Much* and it stood out as if Bonnie Fuller had written it just for me. And then it hit me: There was no reason why I couldn't envision and create my own version of my own world, live in abundance, do what I loved, find peace and joy and love and lots of it. This concept has been burned in my brain since I first read Fuller's book in 2008, and no longer being fearful of having much too much is what has consistently fueled my inner desire to live my best life no matter the circumstances.

On the business side, things quickly (!) turned around when I jumped on the social media train. Unlike naysayers in my industry who proclaimed Twitter and Facebook as a fad, I saw these new platforms as an incredible opportunity to market myself and my travel knowledge to strangers wanting help with their travel plans.

If you build it they will come has never held so true, as it did for me when I branded myself literally overnight to thousands via a blog and social media accounts as *@EliteTravelGal*. I started engaging with my new digital acquaintances and answering questions they had about luxury travel. When my followers (including a favorite TV star and one of the first employees at a major tech firm) called me to book their trips, and then referred their friends and told their large digital followings about me, things began to shift.

On New Year's Eve of 2011, I created a vision board with the intent of manifesting exactly what I wanted (abundance, happiness, health, travel, fun, joy, peace, love). I stared at it daily and prayed to whoever was listening. I also felt grateful that I was attracting new clients and no longer struggling to pay my rent. I stopped freaking out, and that's when everything seemed to miraculously turn around, with regards to business anyway.

After 15 years as a travel journalist/magazine editor, I was on a new path to become one of the first luxury travel agents to build a multi-million-dollar business from home. My target clients didn't care if I worked from my home office. I won an award from my peers for being the country's "Most Innovative Travel Advisor" in 2013. By now, social media was definitely not a fad, but an effective marketing tool that spoke to both my inner journalist and the entrepreneur in me. I got the message loud and clear: Someone needs to target the younger, new generation of luxury travelers. *WHY NOT ME?!?*

Business was booming, but on a personal note, my life was still pretty hellish. I was in a deep dark place when my mom died in 2014. As a now successful business owner with clients worldwide, I was expected to operate as a normal functioning human. The truth? I was a MESS and I had no idea how to function as an adult orphan. I could barely get out of bed, I was crying nonstop and I lost interest in nearly everything except my rescue dogs and getting through the day. I enlisted my best friend to help support my clients and run the business so I could confront the reality of my messy life.

I knew in my soul that I had to consciously choose to heal from the grief that felt unshakeable at the time. I had to accept offers from friends and concerned colleagues to let them help me during this scary time. But, ultimately, I had to help myself.

I made the decision to attend a Deepak Chopra meditation retreat in 2016 on Maui after a similar experience at the Chopra Center in Carlsbad kick-started my major inner-shifts. While meditating twice-daily with Deepak and his daughter Mallika on the topics "What do You Want? What are Your Deepest Desires" it was impossible to ignore the messages telling me to manifest myself a house on Maui. It's where I felt the safest, the most peaceful and the most productive.

I just kept envisioning it happening and knew that it would. What I didn't know is that two weeks later I'd be signing a lease on a house in Pa'ia on the island's north shore, with a rainbow overhead to signify my mom's presence and instead of questioning how I'd swing two houses, I just went with the "Why not me?!?" approach. Why shouldn't I ditch my fancy wardrobe and stressful LA lifestyle for sundresses, flip-flops and the beach? Why shouldn't I have more than one home? Why shouldn't I bring three dogs to Hawaii with me? Someone has to live the life of their dreams, WHY NOT ME?!?

I wasn't planning to quit my day job (not an option as the company CEO!) but I did foresee delegating more to my team, giving myself the time and space to heal properly from the trauma of losing both parents in their 60s to cancer and just really living by the "Why Not Me?!?" mantra.

When I let go of the controls—or as my coach Nancy Levin likes to remind me, resigned as GM of the Universe—everything started to flow. My health improved immensely as I made self-care a full-time priority; my business had its best year ever; and my ability to embrace the mess that is life and live my best (double) life in a way that inspires others to do the same is what prompted me to write this book sharing what I learned on Mother Maui.

Spending a year on an island taught me a lot about living my dreams, and the need to surrender to what I thought "real life" was supposed to look like, especially as a single woman in my 40s. In the peaceful setting of Maui's north shore, I called on angels for guidance and help; I set intentions; I learned to forgive (everyone, including myself); I surrendered to the present instead of worrying about what the future held; and honestly, have never been happier or more at peace—despite having less than zero clue about what comes next.

My happy ending has nothing to do with anyone else (I'm still working on manifesting my big true love of this lifetime), but it's about finding the joy to create my own version of my life story and living it. Despite losing both parents, getting sick, struggling to pay bills and failing a few times in the romance department, I've still managed to master the skill of "Choosing Joy" daily. We all can if we delete whatever is not working well and commit instead to peace, love and happiness as the ultimate set of life goals.

Why Not Me?!? is the compilation of 12 lessons shared in individual chapters about what I learned by taking a year off from the "real" world, which to me, felt anything but real. In realizing that I'm not cut out to live a predictable or boring life, I also accept that I'm not meant to be just in California or Maui but rather, my heart and soul crave and need both! As the eighth tattoo I got during my time on Maui spells out on my ankle for the world to see: It's an infinity sign embedded with the words *CaliGirl* and *IslandTime*. It serves as a reminder that living a life that feels good and right to me all around is honestly all that matters. Someone has to do it, so WHY NOT ME? And, WHY NOT YOU?

PS: I LOVE music. It lifts my vibe, soothes my soul, and just makes me happy. So, in the spirit of sharing what I've learned, I'm including recommended songs themed after each lesson to play and enjoy whenever you need a dose of whatever resonates for you at this time.

For starters, here are the songs I've included in my **Why Not Me Playlist** (it will make sense after you read the book!). You can find and follow all of my book-themed playlists on Spotify under my profile name @elitetravelgal.

Enjoy!

1: Do Life Big, by Jamie Grace
2: Life is Good, by India.Arie
3: Have a Little Faith, by Michael Franti & Spearhead
4: You Better Believe, by Train
5: Not Lonely, Just Alone by Chloe Gilligan
6: Born to Win, by Five for Fighting
7: Like the World is Going to End, by Ben Rector
8: Don't Stop Believin', by Journey
9: Just Do You, by India.Arie
10: This Moment, by Katy Perry
11: Brave, by Sara Bareilles
12: Story of Your Life, by Five for Fighting
13: Rainbow, by Kesha
14: GRATEFUL, by Better than Ezra
15: My Best Days Are Ahead of Me, by Danny Gokey
16: On Top of The World, by Imagine Dragons
17: Maui Cruiser, by Barefoot Natives

18:   You Gotta Be, by Des'ree

19:   Somewhere Over the Rainbow, by Israel Kamakawiwo'ole

20:   Bringing it Home, by Barenaked Ladies

21:   Rise Up, by Andra Day

22:   Hawaii Aloha, by Faith Rivera

23:   Still Standing, by Michael Franti & Spearhead

24:   A Brand New Life, by Panama Wedding

LESSON 1

You Can't Stop the Waves but You Can Learn to Surf

For as long as I can remember, I wanted to learn to surf. Maybe it was growing up in cold, snowy upstate New York where I first fantasized about living closer to the beach, surfing big waves and sunning myself on the warm sand rather than on our blacktop driveway while doused in baby oil, laying out on a cheap chaise with a few sheets of tin foil underneath for extra tanning possibilities. We were just happy to pretend we were somewhere exotic. We made the best of the weather and my dreams of surfing were just that: dreams. Forget the fact that the ocean terrified me, this was something I discovered (and overcame) during my time on Maui.

I learned the meaning of surfing the waves of life however, at a young age. My dad sold jeans throughout most of my childhood. He traveled with racks of clothes in his car trunk to show to buyers at local stores. But mostly, he worked from home and our basement doubled as his sample storage room as well as his office and our playroom. We loved having my dad around, and my stay-at-home mom did the books for his business. As I got a little older, I understood this meant that she was the family money manager. I was also led to understand that life was like the ocean with rolling waves that weren't always predictable. As in, sometimes we had enough money according to my mom, and sometimes not enough. My mom let it be known she didn't agree with my dad's choice to remain in commission-based sales, with lots of uncertainty but more freedom and higher income potential, than for him take a stable but boring nine-to-five managerial role with a lower, albeit, steady paycheck.

I was given a firsthand experience in learning to ride the waves of uncertainty at 14 when our planned vacation to Puerto Rico was abruptly canceled. My dad's biggest account had just filed for bankruptcy and wouldn't be paying their bills which meant the family income (and vacation budget) took a huge hit. Flights were canceled, my parents apologized and said we'd learn to surf some other time, maybe later that summer. Suffice it to say, I was livid that we had to stay home for the holidays. I'd been dreaming of a few days at the beach, surfing and suntanning. Alas, I was expected to just roll with it, and accept that disappointments like this were part of our ups-and-downs-filled life. "Some years are better than others," my mom said, not exactly hiding her own disappointment.

I eventually got over it, but I never forgot the sting of being let down when things didn't go as planned. Ironically, these experiences didn't steer me to seeking out a life of stability in the income department. Like my dad, I wanted the freedom to set my own hours and an unlimited opportunity to generate revenue. When I moved to Los Angeles at 28—with a senior title and a 50K annual paycheck—I soon realized that the ceiling for my chosen editorial career was maxing out at 60K. Instead of just settling for that, I started pitching magazines for freelance writing jobs on the side. I worked on these assignments at night, and soon had generated enough extra income to feel confident enough to quit my day job at age 30. Within a few months, I had far surpassed my monthly income expectations and goals and never looked back. Working for myself, on a project-to-project basis, and later, running a commission-based luxury travel business, is what has truly taught me the meaning of learning to ride the waves.

As a business owner, you never know what each day will bring. As a travel business owner, this is especially true as politics, weather, economics and health crises like swine flu and Zika can damage existing and potential sales overnight. That said, the thrill of being an entrepreneur with endless potential to earn money doing what I love has always allowed me to "surf" the waves. "The only way not to drown is to learn to ride the waves," says Deepak Chopra.

Franky, I've experienced never-ending cycles of waves in my life, on all levels. All of my grandparents passed away before reaching 80. My parents died in their 60s. Several cousins, aunts, uncles, friends were diagnosed at young ages with various diseases and I've watched their struggles end sadly.

Riding these waves has deepened my resolve to live my life differently while learning to process grief and manage stress and not let the waves of life crush me. My mom never learned to surf the waves of the world, but she was like a mermaid in the ocean. She was always the first one to jump into the freezing waters at Nauset Beach on Cape Cod during our summer vacations. Those waves scared the shit out of me. They were huge. Ironically, I'm the one left standing with the skills and strength to literally learn to surf. When I opted to relocate to Maui for a while, it was finally an opportunity to literally learn to surf ocean waves instead of fearing them. It was time to put those childhood dreams into action.

When I found myself dating a surfer on Maui, I thought I'd hit the jackpot. This guy totally wanted to teach me how to surf and stand-up paddleboard. On our first date, despite my fears, we discussed him getting me out on the water. Our next date actually took place in rocky waters on a very windy day (not the type of conditions conducive for a beginner). He told me to lie down on the board when waters got rough promising he'd get us safely to shore. And, he did. But what I realized months later, after ending the short-lived relationship, is that I want someone to ride the waves of the ocean *and* life with me. I want to be with the guy I will learn from, not the one who is just going to tell me to lie down on my board and let him handle things. He ignored my sheer fear of the ocean and failed to show me how to properly use the paddle, which gave me no choice but to let him handle getting us safely to shore.

If nothing else, this failed attempt at learning to "surf" on a day with sub-optimal conditions further spurred my desire to master my fear of the ocean. It also motivated me to achieve my bucket-list goal of catching waves while standing up on a surfboard.

One day, while standing by the shore watching world-class surfers at famous Ho'okipa Beach, I had this nagging sense that my fear of the ocean and the waves was bigger than me. I brought it up with my psychic energy healer that afternoon and she immediately knew what was causing my illogical fear of the ocean. Without hesitation she informed me that I'd drowned in a recent past life, I'd been pushed off a boat by my romantic partner in a traumatic way, so much so that it carried over and translated into a deep fear of the ocean in this lifetime. I was a bit shocked to learn this but it also gave me a sense of relief. As a believer in karma and past lives, I now felt clear on why I was so uncomfortable in the ocean.

Rather than let that deter me from pursuing my learn-to-surf goals, we started with daily healing sessions at the beach. We worked on meditating and clearing my fear while taking baby steps into the gentle surf. A week later, I surprised my healer and I by walking out deep enough to submerge under the water. I rode the rolling waves back into shore. I felt cleansed and healed and knew it was time to schedule surf lessons with a local instructor I'd heard great things about.

Fast forward to the end of that year: I'd taken several surf lessons and had the thrill of standing up on a longboard with my best friend and our incredibly patient teacher. I found the entire process—even just the paddling out to the deeper seas to wait for the right wave—to be fun and cathartic and healing. It was a simple yet powerful metaphor for all I've experienced in life that has forced me to ride the waves over and over and over. A friend who grew up on Maui told me that one of the things they teach kids there is never to turn your back to the waves. That's pretty sound advice. Face the waves, no matter how big, dive in and go under the water if you must. But, never turn your back and pretend the wave doesn't exist. That will never end well. I laughed when he told me this as I'd recently made that mistake while at the beach with friends. I was standing in relatively shallow water but underestimated the power of the waves and got knocked on my ass. It was enough to keep me away from the waves for a few months, but not enough to deter me from my goal of learning to surf.

When things in life get rocky, as they will always do, the choice is always mine to roll with the waves, face them and surf through the process rather than run away from it or freak out over something I cannot control. This strategy serves me well, and it's why nearly everyone on Maui knows how to swim and surf. It is part of the culture to swim and play in the ocean and that means learning to surf, literally. You can't control the waves but you CAN learn to surf.

Surf the Waves Playlist/Lesson 1 Songs:

1: Surfer Girl, by The Beach Boys
2: SURFBOARD, by Cody Simpson
3: Surf's Up, by Brian Wilson
4: Just Say Yes, by Ken Andrews
5: Beautiful Beat, by Nada Surf
6: Walk on the Ocean, by Toad the Wet Sprocket
7: Learning to Fly, by Tom Petty
8: Emoji of a Wave, by John Mayer

LESSON 2

Anything is Possible
When You Believe

Growing up in small town Rochester, New York as a nearly straight-A student and accomplished athlete, I was a type-A perfectionist even as a high-school teen. I loved the rush of being successful at whatever I set my mind to, and I never wanted to disappoint my parents, coaches and teachers, all who imprinted me with the belief that I truly could be whatever I wanted to be. I also recall my mom telling me I should always consider my options (i.e., college, career, boyfriends) and choose to do whatever made me happiest.

I knew at a very early age that I wanted to write for magazines when I grew up; writing made me happy. An introverted kid who preferred reading to socializing if given the choice, it was in second grade when I started voraciously reading my mom's *Woman's Day* and *Family Circle* magazines and whatever "adult" books she left lying around. I was always jotting down my own stories in notebooks and reading magazines whenever possible. Even though it was a financial burden for my family, they agreed to support my choice to pursue a magazine journalism major at Syracuse University's Newhouse School once I got accepted into this prestigious program (early decision, no less!).

My parents told me often they had no idea how they'd afford the private university tuition, yet they still allowed me to pursue my dream of becoming a journalist. I didn't let their financial concerns dampen my excitement about going to one of the country's top journalism schools. I believed I was on the right path and I'd do my part to make my chosen career happen. I took a part-time job waiting tables during college in between journalism classes and I sent $100 a month to the company that never failed to remind me about the student loans no one told me I had signed up for.

After college I wasn't exactly sure where I was headed, but I took a summer job waiting tables in Washington, DC with friends. When that restaurant shut down abruptly, my life path was altered in a way I'm forever grateful for. When the restaurant owner was arrested for tax evasion, it seemed like a sign to start the "real" job search.

A favorite professor had given me a copy of a magazine before graduation and I looked up the phone number of the assistant editor who was a former student of his. When she answered the phone (there was no email or texting back then!), I asked her if she needed an intern. She said, "Yes, when can you start?" I nearly dropped the phone. But first, I let her know I'd be there the next day and I happily accepted the $6 per hour internship (and found myself another waitressing job at nights to be able to pay my bills).

When this internship at *Caribbean Travel & Life* magazine led to a junior editor job (for $17,000 per year!) and plum assignments to visit and write about new hotels (including Richard Branson's Necker Island!), it was my first serious encounter with what Deepak Chopra defines as "synchrodestiny." I truly believed that being a published magazine writer was my destiny, and "synchrodestiny is what happens when what we envision happening comes to fruition." Seeing my byline on articles in magazines on the newsstand was a dream come true, and validated what I knew about being on the right path.

My next job involved a move to Manhattan and a fun but busy job at a weekly travel trade covering hotels and airlines. In my mid-20s, I was barely making enough to pay rent on a tiny studio apartment but I was leading an exciting life traveling around the globe to interview airline CEOs, preview new hotels, attend and write about important travel industry events like the launch of the Star Alliance in Frankfurt, Germany. That notion I had at seven years old that I'd be scoring bylines in major magazines soon became a reality. Seeing my name in print in fitness, health and travel magazines was one of my first lessons in what happens when you believe… in yourself and in your abilities, but also in the universe and what happens when you set intentions and trust they will manifest into reality.

Looking back, these seem like pretty crazy messages to mix into the same head that I now also see was being filled with negative chatter about life "not being fair" and constant fears of what was coming next. This sums up my childhood with a typical Jewish mom who told me she had my best interest and happiness at heart, but who also made me feel guilty for choices she defined as "selfish."

For example, there was that time I asked my boss for a transfer from our New York City office to our Los Angeles office in 1998 simply because I knew I'd be happier in Southern California than in busy, cold New York City. My mom immediately questioned why I would want to move so far away from my family. My time on Maui—and decades of therapy—answered this question: I had to distance myself from negativity and limiting beliefs in order to follow my dreams and stay true to the "anything is possible" theory I intuitively felt drawn to.

Nothing about this theory felt easy during those years filled with challenges ranging from financial stress to traumatic and life-changing losses of friends and loved ones. Before I had my spiritual awakening and took time on Maui to make sense of what made no sense, it felt like everything around me was just falling apart. For a long, long time, my life felt anything but joyful.

At that time, it could have been easy to believe that nothing was fair in my life. My healthy, active young dad got diagnosed with cancer at 59 and died at 63. Then my mother passed away after battling breast cancer for 18 years. At some point, I just stopped focusing on what felt totally unfair, and started to face the reality of what was happening. THIS was the game-changer. Whatever didn't make sense no longer mattered to me because I deepened my belief in the theory that everything does happen for a reason, even without knowing what the reason is at the time. A year on Maui confronting all of my fears (can you say abandonment issues?) left me with this: No matter what I might think while something is happening, life happens FOR me, not TO me. Even when I watched my mom take her last breath, it was this excruciating cracking of my heart that led me to the island. This was a place where I needed to be in a quiet, peaceful space to heal my deepest scars and get back on the track to joy, peace and self-love.

I had to get back on track with believing that anything was possible, in spite of deep emotional scars, poor health, low energy, high anxiety and other obvious symptoms of post-traumatic stress.

At times, I was a total skeptic in the "anything is possible" theory. Who am I to be able to set intentions, envision change and transform my life, letting it flow in the direction I wanted it to go? On the flip side, how could I NOT believe in my powers of manifestation when I started visualizing homes I wanted to live in and they showed up quickly (in Los Angeles, Maui and San Diego). When I visualized a rescue dog I hoped to find someday and a similar one showed up the next day on my Instagram feed of a nearby shelter, I had to embrace the magical powers of manifestation.

I deepened my level of belief in the power of belief during morning walks and meditations on Maui. This gave me the space and time I needed to break away from old messages and current clutter that was taking up too much bandwidth. Clearing it out, letting go and being okay with not knowing what I even wanted to believe led me to return to California with heightened awareness of how powerful our beliefs are. If I think something good will happen, it does. I literally think about an old friend and inevitably receive a text or call from that person. I see numbers 1 and 2 all of the time, on license plates and on hotel rooms I'm "randomly" assigned and it's reassurance that I'm on the right path no matter how screwy life may seem at that given moment. I look up and say thank you to whoever is guiding me along this path, and keeping me laser-focused on my belief in the power of being a believer.

I know for sure that the day of my mom's death is when I hit the point of no return in terms of my belief in a higher power, angels and the guidance that comes from unexpected sources that make it impossible NOT to believe. We (my aunt, sister and I) had made the conscious decision to turn off of my mom's ventilator at exactly 11:22am on 2/2 as she had shared with me years ago that she knew there was something special about the numbers 1 and 2. They appear in each of our birth dates, and my dad's death was on 11/22. When I did the numerology math and realized 2/2/2014 was a number 2 day, the signs were like neon lights to intervene on the day I know my mom would have chosen to exit this world had it been up to her.

And, knowing what I know now, I believe with zero doubt that she chose to depart this world so she could be free of her physical pain and exist as my angel from above.

During my mom's last few days in the hospital, I heard what she was telling us loud and clear even though she was in a coma and unable to speak. I felt her kindly ask me to please take care of Romeo, the pup I had rescued for her five years prior, and I assured her I would. I know she heard me, and trusted I would give him an amazing next chapter with me in Los Angeles. Within days of being at my house in LA, Romeo gravitated toward the afghan my mom had crocheted for me, and it remains his favorite blanket. It keeps me believing in the power of soul-to-soul connection as I witnessed Romeo connect with the one item in my house across the country that had been infused with my mom's energy. It was, and still is, pretty magical and a powerful reminder not to ever stop believing.

Within days of saying our final goodbye to my mom, I started seeing our magic numbers 1 and 2 everywhere. I had never noticed so many gold Toyota highlanders (the car she drove and loved) and I couldn't ignore her favorite song "Somewhere Over the Rainbow" playing nearly everywhere I went. I hadn't quite delved into my spiritual practice yet, but I felt the pull toward seeking peace in a way that was much different than seven years earlier when my dad died and I turned to antidepressants to numb the pain. This time, I felt a connection to my mom even at her deathbed that gave me the strength to seek peace and grief relief in a different way, ultimately through high doses of self-care, meditation, hypnotherapy, and lots of time on Maui.

At 4:12 a.m. on the day of my mom's passing, I abruptly sat up in my hotel bed—which had a window view to the hospital—and I broke into a cold sweat. I can recall that out-of-body experience like it happened yesterday. I got out of bed quietly so I wouldn't wake up my then-boyfriend. In the shower, I cried incessantly while dousing myself with the lukewarm hotel water, as if to wash off the sadness, grief, shock and anger that was already filling my every pore. After nine days of praying to God for my mom to return to her healthier self, I had surrendered to the truth. My mom's soul had clearly left her body, and my body was feeling the pain even though we still had to go say our final goodbyes in a few hours.

While lying in bed waiting for the horrendous events of the day to unfold, I got a text message from an old friend who I hadn't talked to in years. She was reaching out to share with me some very intense and specific messages from my mom, who had asked her to pass them along to me. This friend stated to me at the time: "I don't know if you believe in any of this stuff, but if you do, I have a message for you from your mom. I'm in LA and can share more with you when you return if you'd like to reach out."

What she told me, after letting me know that my mom's soul had left her body around 4 a.m. (!) resonated in a way that shook me to the core. I became a hardcore believer in that moment. And, I've never looked back. I know without a shred of doubt that ANYTHING IS POSSIBLE, when you BELIEVE.

Fast forward to two years later: I found myself spending a year on Maui in a house that I envisioned and manifested after a week of meditating at an island retreat with Deepak Chopra themed around Living with Intention. Suffice it to say, that pushed me over the edge of belief, especially when the house appeared like a mirage at the perfect time in the perfect location at the budget I'd hoped for with a fenced-in yard for my pups. The rainbow overhead and the pink flag flying out front sealed the deal for this believer who's never looked back or questioned why I was led to Maui. I know that my parents had a hand in pushing me to see the signs to go where I could find peace at the time

I needed it most. I wasn't enjoying being an orphan in crazy, busy LA where everyone needed and wanted me all the time. I needed a big fat break, and believing that I could swing a second house on Maui without freaking out about how it would happen is exactly how it happened.

Nothing surprised me during my time on Maui. Not the insanely beautiful rainbows—often double ones—that would appear as if on cue anytime I thought about my parents. The license plates that often showed me my mom's birthday—722—to let me know that she was around always made me smile. Driving by a park called Rainbow Park for the first time and then hundreds of times after never failed to light me up. The Pacific Cancer Foundation event I was invited to at the last minute on the eve before the 10th anniversary of my dad's death was another reminder of synchrodestiny. I wasn't sure I wanted to go solo but I did, and found myself dancing with my tablemates to the local entertainer's rendition of "Forever in Blue Jeans" which was my dad's all-time favorite Neil Diamond song. I found myself saying yes to taking tennis lessons, something my mom always nagged me to do when I never showed any interest. I took daily walks by the ocean just to say hello to the turtles I know were always a sign of my mom's presence. My dad's presence showed up in the form of yellow butterflies that would typically fly by while I was marveling at the immense size and slow motion of the turtles in the sand.

My belief in the power of belief has only strengthened since relocating back to California, where I witness something way too coincidental to be random on a daily basis. I no longer feel shocked or surprised by how often numbers, rainbows, songs and other signs show up. It's comforting in the best way to know that the license plate in front of me with the "XO LIFE" and a pink breast cancer ribbon let me know my mom was joining me and supporting me on the journey that led to my home-buying process. She was witness to my not-so-great experience with this over a decade ago in South Florida, but I feel her pushing me to explore the options and place roots in San Diego, where my business and personal life are flourishing. I also felt my dad show up several times in the form of butterflies. It's impossible for me to miss the signs, and anyone who lives on an island knows that it's much easier to believe that everything is going to be all right than to dare think of the alternative. Casual acceptance of this is the way of life on Maui, and it has played a pivotal role in shifting my former scaredy-cat, stressed-out approach to how things will unfold to one that keeps me rooted in peace, faith, trust and a knowingness that anything truly is possible when you believe.

Believe Playlist/Lesson 2 Songs:

1: Believe, by Cher
2: I Believe, by SOJA with Michael Franti and Nahko
3: You Better Believe, By Train
4: Believer, by Imagine Dragons
5: True Believers, by Darius Rucker
6: I Believe, by Blessid Union of Souls
7: Daydream Believer, by The Monkees
8: Think it, Dream it, Believe it, Do it, by Karen Drucker

LESSON 3

Peace is the Word

"Anything that costs you your peace is too expensive" is one of my all-time favorite mantras, because it's so damn true. My year seeking peace on Maui taught me this, and not in the easiest way. It was a year filled with ups and downs in terms of letting people into my life who threatened my boundaries and compromised my peace levels. At times, it felt like my world was being seriously rocked. When I found myself caught up in turbulent situations, like the wrong relationship, I had to get back to "Anything that costs you your inner peace is too expensive." I said it over and over and over. My peace and joy topped the list of what I needed to bring back into my life after months of turmoil.

No matter how much I meditate or focus on self-care and stress reduction, my ability to stay calm amidst the chaos is a daily challenge. Busy freeways and indecisive clients are a reality in my world, and I have to let go of what I can't control and breathe through the challenges. Like that day I lost my passport just days before an upcoming international trip, and when I discovered my newly rescued pup wouldn't stop howling when I left the house (no one told me he had severe separation anxiety).

At the end of the day, none of these scenarios are earth-shattering nor are they unfixable. They are just annoying and have the ability to shake up my calm quotient if I let them. I'm a first-world problem solver after all.

None of these situations need to affect my inner peace, and they only do if I choose to let them. I can always turn on soothing or upbeat music, chill with my pups or call a favorite friend to vent. Dialing down the non-essential stressors before they truly affect my inner peace is something else I brought back to the mainland with me from Maui. Most people on Maui live by the "peace out" sign-off, as in, stay peaceful, be peaceful, don't let anything unimportant get in the way of you finding and enjoying a peaceful day, a peaceful life.

Committing to staying peaceful in a world that's often anything but is a huge undertaking and requires consistent work-in-progress dedication to the goal. I've been working on mastering inner calm via meditation and stillness now for years. Days when my peace feels rocked are what inspire me to create my own sanctuary—despite the outside distractions—to retreat to, as every good empath needs to do.

As a highly sensitive empath in a loud and busy world, I know when I need to call off plans, write, read, meditate, go to the beach, talk to my coach, nap or resort to doing nothing but resting as a means to refuel my inner peace tank. This requires focus and commitment to peace above everything; no one else has the power to screw up my own inner peace but it does often feel that way when I'm a bit overwhelmed with life.

Keeping inner peace at the top of my short list of priorities in San Diego is a challenge I am up for because my health and happiness and productivity depend on it. Think about it: How can you live your best life and manifest your dreams if you're not in a place of calm and grounded in peacefulness? As my own case study, I decided to test out what I encourage others to do; that is, say no to anything that isn't contributing to a higher level of peace and joy.

One Sunday I was in need of peace and calm, so I opted out of a 45-minute drive to attend services at my favorite spiritual center because I knew I could view the session on Facebook live from my couch! This meant gifting myself an entire day away from everyone, with just my rescue dogs dousing me in puppy love. Once I decided to give myself the gift of this peaceful time, I fully slipped into relaxation mode, taking deep breaths and infusing myself with reiki while visualizing and silently repeating my most favorite Louise Hay affirmation: "All is well. I am safe."

I am so in tune with my need for inner peace because I had been engaged to a narcissist who often yelled loudly to make his point. I had also spent years not setting boundaries with people I dated or lived with. I am a much happier, kinder, healthier and more fun version of myself when I create and stick to boundaries that protect my energy field and give me time to restore and recharge before re-entering the not-so-peaceful reality we live in day in and day out.

Being peaceful is a lifestyle choice that I have put atop my list of what is most important to me. When my inner peace is out of alignment, I am not my best self. Simple as that. The only way for me to be available as my best self for others who need and want my support and time is to be at peace. That means feeling grounded, centered and not on edge with frayed nerves which are a byproduct of too little quiet time and not enough sleep. I know myself well enough to know how important peace is to my health and wellness and happiness, but it's not always easy to explain to friends and colleagues and guys asking me on dates on days I prefer (and need) solitude.

For years, I wasn't acutely aware of the importance of peace in my life because I never truly knew the meaning of it. I grew up in a household with a lot of yelling; I was told what to do and where to be, and often had my brief moments of peace and quiet interrupted by a mom who didn't bother to knock before entering.

We were a "close" family, meaning that lack of privacy and close quarters were standard practice. We shared one upstairs bathroom amongst four of us, and when we traveled, we stayed in one hotel room where I would share a bed with my younger sister. It was anything but peaceful. I went along with it because it was our family dynamic, but I was a kid with a highly sensitive soul that ached for quiet time.

It took me decades to uncover what was at the root of my need for peace and quiet, and why places like airports, Vegas, concerts and shopping malls make me want to jump out of my skin. I just really love peaceful, Zen-like settings that do not threaten my inner calm. I have learned how to breathe and meditate through most situations involving noise and crowds, especially since I am in the travel business and it is part of the world I navigate for myself and others. When I have downtime, I am usually at home in San Diego or spending time on Mother Maui recharging for the next round of life. I live in a place that I love, and I chose my new home for its peaceful vibes and overall sense of sheer calm. The Zen-like garden with a water fountain in the back yard, the ocean location and the gated community, which lends an air of security and safety, all fit my needs perfectly. I feel totally at peace and grounded, and of course, that's always been the ultimate goal.

Ironically, my new home in Carlsbad is just minutes from the Chopra Center where I attended my first "Spirit of Seduction" retreat in November, 2015. Back then, I was still numb from my mom's death and hadn't yet come to terms with how to end the wrong relationship or where to go once I awoke from the fog I'd been cruising along in. A week with Deepak led me to start questioning "What do I want? What are my deepest desires?" Just one month later, I ended the three-year long-distance relationship I had been pretending to enjoy. I started to feel light and free, and I know my week in Carlsbad at the Chopra Center was the beginning of this path to peace I ultimately desired and deserved.

Peace isn't something reserved for people who don't experience trauma or life challenges; it's a lifestyle open and available to anyone willing to take a close look at what's causing pain, delete toxicity on all levels and commit to putting peace on the top of the priority list.

Shortly after that long-distance relationship had ended, I traveled to Maui solo to attend another Chopra Center retreat. This one was themed around "Living with Intent" and was billed as a tribute to Dr. Wayne Dyer, who also lived on and loved the island I felt called to. I craved the deep peace I had felt on prior visits to Maui, so I gave myself the gift of a few extra days at a luxury hotel on the beach to reground and center myself before the Deepak retreat. I hadn't been feeling well, and I truly needed a break from the daily grind. Maui was going to be a much-needed dose of peace. I was prepared to tune out, tune in and listen to my inner voice with as little outside distraction or noise as possible.

That plan worked for about a day, until my assistant texted me that longtime clients were panicked when they realized—at the airport on the way to an international vacation we'd been planning for months— that the kids' passports were expired. This was a bigger "crisis" than my assistant could handle on her own without my guidance, so my plans for a peaceful lazy vacation day turned into hours nonstop of rapid-fire emails, texts and plan adjustments. After years of practice in first-world problem solving, I was able to reschedule their Europe trip for months later. I called in favors and got them rooms at a sold-out Hawaiian resort, booking them flights for the next day. This way, they wouldn't need passports but would still get to enjoy their spring break vacation.

I'll never forget how annoyed I felt at having to sacrifice my much-needed peace of mind in order to be the hero on the work front that day. I felt I had no choice but to drop my own plans to take care of the work situation that arose unexpectedly. While changing lives through travel is what I do for a living, I needed more than just work to be the center of my life. I wasn't feeling well, my nerves were frayed, my stress level was still in that post-grief range of way too high, and I was truly craving a disconnection (if only temporary) from my "I run a luxury travel company" identity.

More than anything, I wanted to remember what it felt like to be at peace. I found myself having little patience for these clients that week, especially when they accused me for not reminding them to check their passport expiration dates. I didn't have it in me to fight them, and I graciously let them know I thought it would be best for them to work with someone else in the future. Peace was emerging as my top priority, and I needed to start deleting people—friends and clients—who compromised my ability to stay in this space. This has been my story ever since; I honestly cannot work with anyone whose emails make me cringe when I see their name appear in my inbox. It's not good for anyone. And, it's not necessary. Peace is, however, very necessary.

In that particular scenario with the vacation-headache clients, I was past the point of enjoying the need to feel needed because honestly, I wanted to be left alone. I had set aside this time and booked this trip with a specific goal and purpose: finding peace in the land of aloha. Later that day, once the crisis had been averted and their trip had been reorganized, I got into my rental Jeep and took a drive to the side of the island I hadn't visited before. I was intrigued by the sound of a town called Haiku so I drove north thinking about how much more peaceful life became once I stepped away from my laptop to enjoy a scenic drive.

I drove under huge trees on Kokomo Road without a clue where it would lead, only to stumble upon the Temple of Peace Healing Center. It was colorfully painted and appeared like a mirage after driving for miles of seeing only the ocean and trees. My jaw dropped because all day I'd been in search of peace and here was an entire temple devoted to peace. What are the odds? Talk about divine timing.

I'd yet to really fully understand my own powers of manifestation but something clicked inside of me that day. I needed peace, I asked for peace, I found peace, literally, on the side of a road I'd never explored before. The Temple of Peace has been on Maui for years, but it was totally unfamiliar to me until that day I really needed a sign that peace was, in fact, just around the corner. I keep that vision with me, and I often drove to that spot during my days on Maui as a reminder that peace is not ever out of reach. Even on challenging days, we can always find our happy peaceful place in the world. This might be a favorite yoga studio or a juice bar or your own bathtub filled with hot water and lots of Epson salt. Some days, the latter is the best I can do if a flight to Maui isn't possible in the moment, but it's a guaranteed way to release any energy that's blocking my sense of peace and calm.

The moral of this lesson is that you can always choose your word that will define how you wish for your life to be. For me, peace is the centerpiece of my world. If I am not at peace, and cannot find ways to restore and recharge my peace when it gets out of balance, I am not living my best life and I can't possibly thrive in today's busy crazy world. So, choose your word. Go to Chris Pan's website *www.MyIntent.org* and order yourself a necklace or bracelet emblazoned with your word. Do whatever you need to do to Live it, Breathe it, Be it. For me, Peace is the Word.

Peaceful Playlist/Lesson 3 Songs:

1: Peaceful World, by John Mellencamp
2: Peaceful Feeling, by Sheryl Crow
3: Peace, by Ben Rector
4: Peace, by O.A.R.
5: Peace Like a River, by Paul Simon
6: Peace Train, by Cat Stevens
7: Peaceful Easy Feeling, by The Eagles
8: Peacekeeper, by Fleetwood Magic

LESSON 4

The Bigger the Storm, the Brighter the Rainbow

For as long as I can remember, I've been obsessed with rainbows. Back in the day (it was the '80s), I had that adorable rainbow-adorned bedspread when it was trendy, and a few funny rainbow tees and sweatshirts. And, I loved it when my mom would sit down at the piano and play her favorite song, "Somewhere Over the Rainbow." She did this often, in hopes that I'd be inclined to stick with piano lessons and get around to playing that rainbow song myself. To her dismay, when given a choice, I opted out of piano lessons and chose soccer and softball as afternoon hobbies. I cared more about making my dad—who encouraged my inner tomboy— proud of my athletic achievements than I did of impressing the piano teacher with bad breath who wanted me to promise to practice daily. It was an obvious no-brainer, even at age 12.

As much as I loved rainbows, I really disliked the rain, thunder, lightning and the resulting messiness that came after a rainstorm—and before the rainbows. Walking dogs (something that's always been a part of my life) was never fun in the rain; no one enjoys dealing with a wet soggy dog who doesn't like being that way. In all honesty, the tie between rainbows and the storms that produce them wasn't quite on my radar until I started spending a lot of time on Maui, and discovered the beauty that came after the rain.

The "over the rainbow" song however, has long been with me, as a genuine reminder of my mom's "hidden" talents and her deep love for this particular tune. It spoke volumes about her outlook on life. She would sing along while playing even though her singing was completely off-key. It didn't matter; she just seemed to get lost in the words, as if they were a premonition of her future path. "Way up high, there's a land that I've heard of, once in a lullaby... Somewhere over the rainbow, skies are blue, and the dreams you dare to dream really do come true... All my troubles melt like lemon drops, way above the chimney tops, that is where you'll find me."

Decades later, when breast cancer had overtaken my mom's body and it was obvious her days were limited, the song held an even deeper meaning. I found myself praying for her to pass away peacefully and float up to the land she'd heard of, where skies are blue and her troubles would all be melted away. And, a few sessions with mediums later, my intuitive hits were confirmed. On multiple occasions, various healers and psychics asked me if the song "Somewhere Over the Rainbow" meant anything to me because it had apparently played in their car or in their head while they were driving to our session. This goes in the "can't make this up" file, and it also validates what I know to be true about the power of belief in a higher power.

Embracing the guidance I've received from psychic mediums, including Denver-based Rebecca Rosen and San Diego-based Sarah Renee, has empowered me to liberate myself from the naïve notion that my parents' departures from this earth after their long painful cancer battles could have been any different. "At 67, your mom's work here was done," the rabbi told us matter-of-factly at my mom's funeral. While it didn't ease or prevent the pain of the loss, it did soften the shock of why everything was unfolding as it was. My mom's time to leave her cancer-ridden body behind in favor of the life she dreamt of "somewhere over the rainbow" had come, and it wasn't up to me to question why.

What was left to me was to make peace with the reality of being abandoned by both parents which qualified me as an orphan. Nothing prepares you for this type of reality. The choice becomes living in denial and failing to process the grief that's inevitably going to hit—hard and often—or finally face it all head-on. In my case, it meant not only confronting and dealing with my own health challenges and unhealed traumas, but also delving deeply into what was unresolved with both parents and addressing all of it.

Anytime I'd see a rainbow or hear the rainbow song—as I did the year my mom died in destinations from Shanghai to Venice to Tokyo—it was like a big colorful reminder that no matter what, my parents' presence was always going to be felt. Taking ownership of my sadness that initially accompanied every sign of my parents' post-death ultimately transformed into a new set of skills that allowed me to consciously choose to put peace and joy atop my priority list while here on this planet.

I decided that I wanted to do life much differently than my mom; I wanted to live the shit out of THIS life and not just fantasize and sing about how great it will all be when living above the clouds, trouble-free "Somewhere Over the Rainbow."

What has truly been empowering has been my own ability to connect the meaning to my mom's presence every time I see a rainbow, or hear the rainbow song, or witness a sign that speaks about rainbows.

But, it was not until I started spending a lot of time on my favorite island of Maui and driving rental cars with rainbows and the "Aloha State" moniker on their license plates (!) did I make the connection that rainbows are the beautiful result from the rains that often douse the tropical island.

I stopped getting sad when the skies would darken, and instead, looked forward to what was about to unfold in the form of a beautiful colorful rainbow or two or three. It got to the point where anytime it was obvious that storms were imminent, I'd just relax into the knowing that pretty soon there would be rainbows upon rainbows, often double ones, just lighting up the skies. It's magical, and humbling in the sense that we can always see the "pot of gold" at the end of the rainbow when we stop focusing on the negative. I swapped my negativity around the rain which often screwed up timing of tennis lessons or canceled beach swims (which both could easily be rescheduled) and found myself becoming like most on the island, saying: "There's no rainbow without the rain."

I eventually just gave in and embraced it. The need to embrace what's out of my control became a constant theme while living on island time, and it's continued to follow me into this next phase of my life where I'm given daily lessons in letting go of what's not within my control.

I still, to this day, do not love rain, but after experiencing the incredible natural beauty of rainbow after rainbow, I don't hate it quite so much. I know that natural beauty is nothing to knock, and I find myself a bit more patient and tolerant of rainy days knowing that over all they are necessary for the health of our environment. Being back in Southern California is a reminder of this, especially during recent times when fires are raging not all that far from my home

Whenever I'm spending time on Maui, I see rainbows light up the sky anytime I find myself thinking of my parents and needing a sign that they're strongly present. When I'm traveling, I often hear the song "Somewhere Over the Rainbow." It used to freak me out when I'd be having cocktails with colleagues in a bar on the Grand Canal in Venice, Italy or attending a business dinner at the fanciest restaurant in Shanghai or watching street performers in Capetown and the entertainers would start singing that tune. The oddness of it turned to comfort as the years have gone on, and now, anytime I hear that song I just smile as I know it's a sign that my mom is with me.

Finding comfort in signs, be it a rainbow or a song, is a significant way to incorporate self-healing into your own life on a consistent basis. Rainstorms, like the recent Hurricane Lane that pummeled Hawaii, remind us that certain things are out of our control but everything is temporary and there is always a beautiful rainbow at the end of every storm.

Rainbow Playlist/Lesson 4 Songs:

1: Somewhere Over the Rainbow, by Israel Kamakawiwo'ole
2: Rainbow, by Kesha
3: Double Rainbow, by Katy Perry
4: Rainbow Connection, by Sleeping At Last
5: Rainbows & Waterfalls, by Pretty Lights
6: Rainbowland, by Miley Cyrus and Dolly Parton
7: She's a Rainbow, by The Rolling Stones
8: Chasing Rainbows, by Bring Me The Horizon
9: No Rain, No Rainbow, by BabyMetal

LESSON 5

Your Family is the Ohana You Choose

Of all the lessons I learned on Maui, this one resonates deeply: The Hawaiians have the right idea when it comes to family. In Hawaiian, the word "ohana" translates literally to "family," but it goes far beyond the traditional definition limiting family to our blood relatives. In Hawaii it is common practice to consciously decide who gets to be part of your ohana and it has nothing to do with the family you are born into. While living on Maui, the grief I'd experienced after losing both parents shifted and dare I say, dissipated, as local friends welcomed me warmly into their families. I experienced the local tradition and beautiful meaning of consciously choosing and creating your own extended family, filled with your closest friends and people whose souls often felt more like family to me than those I share DNA with. The concept of "soul family" started to make sense as I connected with people on Maui at a deeper level than I'd ever felt with my own blood relatives.

This started to make sense when I said yes to the invite to spend Thanksgiving at the home of a now close friend I consider a soul sister. She was one of my first friends on Maui, and shortly after we met I learned she was heading off-island for a double mastectomy. When we met, those special friendship sparks flew, as if the universe threw us together for reasons neither of us were supposed to understand. I'd recently lost my mom to breast cancer, my best friend Alyson had recently beaten it, and this new friend of mine who looked like one of the healthiest, strongest women I'd ever met was dealing with the disease too. I gave my friend reiki (mastered on the island after feeling the call to do so) the night before her surgery. She was grateful to my newfound healing skills, and I was so very grateful that she'd invited me to her home for the holiday that triggers all my emotions due to the timing (my dad passed away the night before Thanksgiving in 2006).

Another time I realized the impact of Hawaiian ohana was when I was sitting on the beach with some new tennis friends. I had met the son of one of the girls only once when he showed up and she said, "Did you say hello to Auntie Stacy?" Her adorable five-year-old turned around, and without giving it any thought, said: "Hello Auntie Stacy." Only in Hawaii did you become part of the ohana with the kids of friends who you recently bonded with over tennis, the beach and cocktails.

The use of "auntie" was common amongst friends who call each other sisters in the tight-knit island community. I'd grown up in a world where your aunts were your parents' sisters, not friends you decided to give that title to. I must say, I loved it. I loved everything about being considered part of my friends' local ohana, and it made me realize that I can totally choose my own ohana as I move through the rest of my life, healed and cleared from the memories of the past. WE ALL CAN.

Recently, my energy healer and I discussed my family and the lingering negative energy that needed to be cleared out of my world.

I often questioned my lack of connection to my Jewish roots. I also wondered why I felt way more at home on the sunny warm west coast than I ever had in upstate New York. Before grasping an understanding of soul contracts (meaning, our souls come into each lifetime with a contract to fulfill), it was inexplicable to me how I could be so different than my only sister and why my parents didn't ever seem to "get" me. I struggled for decades with trying to fit myself into the family mold I was born into.

As kids, unbeknownst to us—and without having a choice—we form limiting and untrue beliefs based on the behavior and conversations we are repeatedly subjected to. What I recall hearing over and over and over during my childhood (and actually, into adulthood until I moved far away) was this: "You have to be nice to your sister" and "Listen to your mother, because Mom always knows best." Not exactly.

I had little in common with my sister and was forced to spend time with her, which didn't work out well for either of us. As adults, my sister and I are still grappling with how we can have a healthy relationship that works for both of us. I've had to set boundaries and she's had to choose if she wants any relationship with me at all based on these boundaries. I'm optimistic we've both evolved to a place of preferring a peaceful co-existence than the non-communication style we tried (and failed at) in the past. Given we are each other's only sibling in this lifetime, it feels better to have a better relationship without the pressures and expectations of how our parents wanted it to be.

And, as for my mom always knowing best, there is zero truth to this. I loved my mom deeply until her death and have made peace with the guilt she was a master at tripping us with, but there was no handbook that taught her everything she needed to know to make her the smartest person on the planet. She married my dad at 19, had me at 23, and had my sister at 25. She told me more than once she wished that someone had told her how hard it (raising a family?!) was going to be. I know she did the best she could, especially when ill, and given her capabilities, but it certainly doesn't mean she was always right. Her emotional outbursts were painful to partake in or be subjected to, as they often seemed unfounded. No one on the outside saw what we did on the inside of my house. This "perfect family" that many perceived us to be was anything but perfect. I wanted out. I wanted freedom from being told how I had to act, especially in the company of my family.

I was often reprimanded (loudly) for stepping outside the boundaries my family tried hard to instill, simply because they didn't feel natural or good or anything close to right to me. I moved far away from all of them when I was 28 and can still hear my mom questioning my decision to head west to Los Angeles as if I was moving to the moon. Now I know why: It was all about her fear of not having me in close proximity. I followed my intuition, as I always knew I had a different kind of life to lead than my east coast family. I hated everything about living and working in New York City and even though I had no clue yet what an empath was (or that I am a textbook one) I knew that I needed to be far, far, far away from all the noise so that I could learn to live on my own terms and actually breathe!

I also always loved my alone time. I've always craved peace and quiet, but my family didn't understand this or respect my needs. I would shut my bedroom door, and someone would open it without knocking. It explains a lot about why I've been challenged to share my space or spend too much time with anyone before needing time out to be alone to recharge. My desire to be independent and free of the family ties that bound me resulted in tough losses on the relationship front. I often chose totally wrong people to let into my life, both romantically and professionally, because at times, I found them easier to deal with than anyone who challenged me. Often, I forgot to set any boundaries, and typically I ignored the very bright red flags.

I had to figure things out as an adult, and I couldn't deal with listening to my mom's constant nagging and questioning of my judgment or criticism that I now know stemmed from her own fear of failure and was not a true reflection of her faith in my abilities to succeed. I didn't know how any of it was going to work. All I knew is that I wanted to break free from the confines of my traditional family and create my own version of my own adult world. I knew that I could do this much more easily if I detached from my DNA relatives, I just didn't have any idea what I was doing at the time when this journey began 20 years ago.

With little money in the bank, but a decent editorial job waiting for me in my magazine's Los Angeles office, I drove across the country in 1998 in a yellow Penske van with my now closest friend and soul sister Alyson. It was Memorial Day weekend and at 28, I felt happier and more free than I had in my entire life. That trip was life-changing as we did what we wanted, ate when we were hungry and planned our own schedule. The night before we hit Los Angeles, we even stayed up all night drinking and dancing with crazy new friends in Vegas. I knew I had to get back to the reality of my trade magazine reporter job starting that week, but it was sheer bliss being far away from family.

I say this now without guilt, without hesitation and with the desire only to share my truth about not having a perfect childhood or the family everyone else thought was perfect. Our blood relatives are not automatically our closest friends, nor do they have to be. We can choose to walk away from toxic family members in the name of putting our own health first; it's just not anything we are taught to do when growing up. We must learn on our own and do so without guilt or shame or fear of what others in our gene pool might say about our choices. Trust me, I've heard it all. I've also had to accept that what's best for me is not for anyone else—in my family or not—to understand. I have a challenging time understanding why some people stay married to spouses they confess to having nothing in common with for the sake of "the family." But, if I've learned nothing else, it's not to judge anyone else's choices and stay focused on choosing to spend time with "chosen family" and whatever will bring me the most peace and joy.

I cherish my tight-knit group of friends and I am careful who I let into my ohana more for my sake than theirs. I love having a community of like-minded, soulful friends but I also need people who bring joy and peace to my life. When you see groups of friends on Maui, you usually cannot tell who is "blood-related," and who is just fortunate to be part of the ohana. Many people I met introduced each other as so-and-so's brother or sister only to later add that they were their "Hanai family" which meant they'd been "informally adopted."

It is a world I feel so lucky to be part of. The connections are made by choice, and out of true friendship and respect, not obligation. I loved feeling part of various ohanas, and back on the mainland am actively practicing choosing who comprises my ohana. While my relationship with my blood sister is still a work in progress, having a soul family that continues to grow reminds me that like attracts like. We are all born into the family we need to learn a LOT from. And, we always have the choice to walk away from toxic relationships, familial or not, and opt into an ohana that feels warm, loving, safe and joyful. The Hawaiians set the best example when it comes to this choosing your family concept. Friends truly are the family you choose.

Family Playlist/Lesson 5 Songs:

1: We Are Family, by Sister Sledge
2: Family Man, by Lily Allen

3: Ode To My Family, By The Cranberries

4: Friends Are Family, by Oh, Hush! Featuring Will Arnett and Jeff Lewis

5: Blended Family, by Alicia Keys

6: Family of Me, by Ben Folds

7: Family Portrait, by P!nk

8: Family Reunion, by Jill Scott

LESSON 6

Dogs, Not Diamonds, are a Girl's Best Friend

If you've ever rescued a dog, you get it. There is nothing that compares to the level of unconditional love that comes packaged in the soul of rescue pups. I say this after nearly 20 years of being a serial dog rescuer. After dousing these rescue dogs with a love they never experienced before, I have also learned the art of receiving the love these dogs offer to me.

Dogs have a unique way of communicating their love, and once we learn to receive it, nothing can break this special bond. During an energy-clearing session, one of my favorite island-based healers, *Hoku on Maui*, suggested to me that as a "dog person" I should practice letting my pups love on me even more. There is always room for more love in our lives, from ourselves, our pups and anyone we open our hearts to. Personally, I was in a challenging growth phase, post-break-up and ready to push forward with my next chapter, and Hoku reminded me to be open to receiving my dogs' limitless love. Unlike people, who find reasons to withhold love all the time, these pups only want to bring us joy over and over. They teach us the importance of not only showering them with love, but letting them do the same for us.

Days before I was set to move in with my then-fiancé, I looked down at my hand, with a tiny band of sparkling diamonds on my left finger, and I cried tears of sadness at my decision to say yes to his proposal three months prior. Within a few months of getting engaged at the local coffee shop where we'd had our first date, I knew I couldn't go through with the wedding. I've always said I only want to get married once in this lifetime. This wasn't going to be a fulfillment of that life plan.

There were too many red flags I couldn't ignore. The stress of the relationship was resulting in sleepness nights, and it was my rescue pups, not my fiancé, who I wanted to share my bed and beach walks with. Some might say this isn't normal, and that I wasn't opening myself up to true love with a human soulmate, but I call bullshit on that. My dogs sensed this human relationship was painful, unsafe and damaging to my soul. When your love for your animals is deeper and stronger than the person who you are supposed to be in partnership with, it's a true sign who belongs and who needs to go.

Once I took the diamond ring off and ended the engagement, I could return to my commitment of finding true love with the right human who would love me as much as my pups did and vice versa. Over the years, my rescue dogs have shown up so many times and gotten me through so many challenging times that it's obvious this is their role in my life.

I've always loved dogs for as long as I can remember. I should probably thank my parents for this as there are vintage photos of me with two toy poodles in my crib days after I was born. Dogs to me are soul-soothers and instant friends. We always had a family pup but it wasn't until I was a grown adult—and I started rescuing dogs on my own—that my understanding of unconditional love and their purpose on this planet truly took form.

My mission to help homeless dogs started when I moved into my first apartment on my own in Los Angeles. I was in the midst of launching my first business and working on it from home because I was recovering from major knee surgery. It was 2000, Google was brand new and being used to find out all sorts of things, including—I learned—rescue dogs! I stayed up for hours scouring the internet for local rescue sites late one night, and stumbled on a gray and white one-year-old Shih Tsu/Bichon available for adoption. The next day, I drove out to Pet Orphans Fund, a rescue facility in the San Fernando Valley. The minute this messy, sweet pup jumped on my lap (after days of being cooped up with multiple bigger and louder dogs), I knew she was meant for me. They were calling her Charity, and I renamed her Madeline after my favorite childhood storybook character. I think even back then I knew I wasn't going to have human children, so I gave her the name I would have given to my first daughter had that been my destiny.

Maddie and I bonded over lots of long walks, which helped me get outside and rehab my knee more than I would have on my own. I took her on long car rides in my convertible up the PCH and loved being a dog mama. It gave me a purpose (and responsibilities) at a level I'd never known before. While sweet and loving with me, Maddie was skittish and barked at people she didn't know along with every cat, and everyone in a uniform like the mailman and the delivery guy. While I worked on lowering her anxiety, which clearly came from past abuse and trauma, she won my heart with her protective nature. She and I were inseparable, especially on the morning of 9/11 when I took her to my friend's house and we all paced the streets of Santa Monica, shattered from the shock but able to take comfort in our canine pals who knew something was wrong and only wanted to make us feel better.

While I loved my LA lifestyle, a surprise move across the country back to New York City showed up a few months later. The magazine I was running was based there, and 9/11 changed everything because my boss felt it would be best for me to be based where the company was (instead of traveling back and forth between coasts). I agreed to the move, thinking it would be a one-year stint. LA would be there for me when it was time to return.

While I wasn't a huge fan of early morning and late-night walks on loud city streets, sweet Madeline never showed signs of caring about the environment as long as we were together. The unconditional love was obvious, as was my inability to live and work in such a busy noisy city after a few years out west. Still thinking it was a temporary stay on the east coast, I moved us out of the noisy Manhattan apartment and into a larger house with a yard 30 minutes away in Greenwich, CT. I did this with Maddie's best interest in mind as much as mine. It was during this time that I received the sad, shocking news that my 59-year-old dad had cancer. I wasn't going back to LA anytime soon. I took Maddie with me on many road trips up to Rhode Island to visit my dad, and I know that she was the reason I was able to make it through some of those very dark days without totally losing my mind.

The cold weather and stressful job running *Elite Traveler* magazine was taking its toll, and the guy I was dating suggested we relocate to West Palm Beach, Florida. This sounded better than staying in the cold northeast, so I agreed to the plan and we headed south, each with a pup we'd had for years. Once settled, I found myself driving to the local animal shelter to volunteer my time. My dad had been in and out of the hospital a lot, and I wasn't handling the stress and sadness of life very well. I was trying my best to grow my new travel business, be a loving partner to my boyfriend I'd recently bought a house with, and figure out how to handle the inevitable ending to my dad's story.

What I didn't expect was to see the most beautiful dog I'd ever seen sitting in a cage at the shelter staring at me as if she'd been waiting for me. Years ago, after seeing a friend's golden retriever puppy, I'd told my boyfriend that a mini-golden would be my "dream dog." Little did I know that this golden girl was my manifestation come true, in the form of a six-year-old fully grown mixed golden retriever/cocker spaniel. There was no doubt she was meant for me, so I named her Riley, took her home, introduced her to Maddie, my boyfriend and his dog Charlie and thanked God daily for this incredibly special dog mom/rescue dog relationship that carried me through my dad's death (five weeks later).

As numb and depressed and traumatized as I was from losing my dad, the realization of how powerful puppy love could be was the silver lining in my life at that time. When I ended my six-year relationship with the guy I had moved to Florida with, I was clear that I didn't care about leaving behind any of our shared belongings, but Riley and Maddie were coming with me back to Los Angeles. They were my angels and all that brought me joy at this time. With little savings, only my computer, my clothes, and these two rescue pups, I left behind my house (that needed to be sold during the Big Short era), my family (mom, sister and nephews) who had recently relocated to Florida and the life I knew wasn't enjoying. I much preferred LA and the west coast lifestyle to NYC or West Palm Beach, and it was time to press on in the company of these pups. Their unconditional love was all I needed to get through six days on the road, solo, a year after losing my beloved dad.

We loved the house I rented for us in the heart of Brentwood, my favorite neighborhood in LA. Those pups licked my face and made me laugh, all the time. We had as much fun as we could while I was struggling to make money and process the deep grief that came along with the reality of my dad's death.

On a bit of a whim, while back in Florida for my birthday and to spend time with my family, I went to a local shelter in search of a lap dog for my mom. Her little pup Mandy has passed away shortly after my dad died, like she was waiting to join him, and I knew my mom—who was grieving deeply and also battling breast cancer—missed having a dog. As if on cue, the cutest six-month-old puppy with funny teeth and a sweet spirit barked at me to come say hi to him. That moment you pick up a homeless dog and he kisses your face like you're his long-lost love, you know he's chosen you as his dog mom. In this case, Romeo was going to have to settle for me as his rescuer but he was being gifted to my mom as I already had two of my own waiting for me back in LA.

It was a sweet love affair for Romeo and my mom, and I couldn't get his cuteness off my mind. So, when I happened to stroll by an adoption fair a few blocks away from my house in LA, the love I had for Romeo translated into me adopting another cute pup for myself (to complement Riley and Maddie). Out of the 25 cute small mixed dogs in the pen, one especially messy, cute, fluffy funny maltipoo caught my attention. The minute I got close to him, he put his paws up, stared at me and I got the message. I'd seen it a few times now: that look of "Please get me out of here. Please take me home." I named him Mikey.

And thus began my journey as a three-dog mom. My heart just continued to expand with the love that these munchkins—as I called them—brought to my life. No matter what kind of shitty mood I was in, or what kind of challenges the business was posing, there were always three souls needing my attention and wanting to douse me with love. A few years later, the story continued with me fostering an adorable but crazy Lhasa puppy I called Bella. She was the only dog I've ever fostered for a year and then handed over to a grateful friend in need of puppy love. Having four dogs was proving to be a bit more than I could handle as a single woman growing a business and traveling a ton, but I happily let my friend adopt Bella because it was the right thing for all of our souls.

The deep painful sadness that came when both Maddie and Riley left my world (Maddie in 2013 and Riley in 2015) was a reminder of how much love can hurt but only because it's such a pure, deep and true love. These sweet pups taught me so much. And, in both cases, it was only a few months before my next angel dog showed up for rescuing. A few days prior to my mom dying, I stood at her hospital bedside and assured her that Romeo would come back to LA with me. I just know it's what she wanted, as if I'd heard the message from above, loud and clear. No one questioned my plan, and a week later, Romeo was west-coast bound to join us. As one of my friends said upon meeting him, "How wonderful that Maddie's role in your life is now being played by Romeo."

This sweet little guy was so connected to my mom after sitting on her lap for five years—and making her laugh with his silly antics—that he's brought that energy into my house in an unmistakable way. He loves everyone who meets him, but no one more than me. We have a special bond and it's a daily reminder of the love that people and pups share which transcends many human-to-human bonds.

Not even four months after the painful loss of Riley, who I always referred to as my "Golden Girl," I was scrolling my Instagram feed and a photo of Riley's doppelganger popped up. It was posted by a local LA adoption group only blocks away from my house, and crazy enough, her shelter name was "Daisy Hope" which immediately caught my attention as my name is Stacy Hope. And, it was a few days before my birthday. I hadn't planned on adopting another dog just yet, but I found myself following my intuition down the street, and on Halloween day,

I met my next golden angel. I named her Holly (short for Halloween Pumpkin) as a reminder of the day we met. It was another case of love at first sight, despite her having kennel cough, ear and eye infections, poor skin and an obvious case of the shelter blues. I was booked to attend my first weeklong Deepak Chopra retreat in San Diego the next day, so she came with me. Talk about moving on up! While sequestered in the peaceful setting at La Costa Resort, we bonded slowly. The sweet staff at the hotel took her on walks while I was in sessions, and even made a run to Whole Foods and the pet store to procure anything we needed for this unexpected journey. It was super sweet and another reminder of how much love even an abused rescue dog has to give. All she needed was love and to feel safe, which is what we all really crave, isn't it?

When I decided to relocate to Maui for a while, there was no question that my trio of pups (Mikey, Romeo and newly renamed golden girl Holly) would join me. It was quite the process, with four-month waiting periods required for dogs to enter Hawaii, and all kinds of tests and paperwork. I never really gave it much thought; I just moved forward with getting everyone cleared. Once on the island, these dogs and I bonded in an even deeper way. They loved barking at the neighboring goats and chickens, and it was constant entertainment. Everyone who met them fell in love with their playful spirits.

Holly had a few health scares, and sadly, passed away while I was on a business trip back on the mainland a night before our two-year anniversary. Ironically, I got the call letting me know while I was dining on pumpkin soup in the pumpkin capital of the world the night before Halloween. Hearing about Holly's death on the night before Halloween while surrounded by pumpkins was comforting in an unexplainable way. It was as if she'd come into my life on a mission, to help me move past the grief of losing Riley and to be reminded of my own manifestation powers. And also, her short time with me was just long enough to teach me a deeper level of patience and compassion as she was never super healthy and always required an extra dose of love and kindness from me.

Holly's death seemed to go unnoticed by Mikey and Romeo who relished the extra attention they were receiving from me. Just when I thought I couldn't love them more, they proved me wrong with their incredible sweetness. They enjoyed being a duo, a pair of look-alike cuties that many mistake for twins. When we left Maui and relocated from LA to San Diego, Mikey and Romeo never seemed fazed by any of the transition. We moved through the airport in Maui, onto the plane, back to my Brentwood apartment (for two weeks), packed that place up and drove two hours south to a townhouse I'd never even seen before but had trusted friends to find for me. Without skipping a beat, we all settled quickly into our lovely new life in San Diego. Long walks to the water with plenty of play time in the park works well for these guys and it also brings me much joy.

Since returning from Maui to the mainland, I was hesitant to add to my brood because life truly felt really easy with just two small and sweet healthy rescue pups. However, as is standard practice for my life, the minute I put out into the universe that I'd be open to welcoming another cocker or golden that needed us, one showed up! It's literally as if I'd snapped my fingers and said, "I'm ready. Who needs us?"

I googled "San Diego cocker spaniel rescue" on a whim and that night, a gorgeous nine-year-old golden-colored cocker popped right up on the San Diego Spaniel Rescue website. I could not get him out of my mind. His eyes were soulful and had that look I'd seen many times: Come get me, please. A day later, I was in the car on my way to adopt him out of his foster home. As I let the universe know I was ready, and bam, my next rescue pup is on its way to me. I named him Pono as in Live Pono (do the right thing). He's my Pono pup and I fell in love at first sight with him. Not a surprise. Rescue dogs are a never-ending source of unconditional love and such incredible teachers of gratitude and patience. The big lesson here is to always, always keep your heart open to finding love as genuine as puppy love.

Dogs, Not Diamonds Playlist/Lesson 6 Songs:

1: Diamond Dogs, by David Bowie
2: Diamonds, by Rihanna
3: Lucy in the Sky with Diamonds, by Elton John
4: Puppy Love, by Joe Taylor
5: True Love, by P!nk
6: Love Myself, by Hailee Steinfeld
7: Love Is My Religion, by Ziggy Marley
8: Love Always Finds a Way, by Karen Drucker

LESSON 7

Fences (and Goats) Make for Great Neighbors

I've learned a lot about being a good neighbor the past few years, both on Maui and in California. For starters, there is nothing like a really great fence to establish boundaries between the people you share a lot line—and sometimes walls—with. When I signed the lease on my first house on Maui, I immediately saw the need to "Fort Knox" the backyard so my pups could roam freely without any reason to fear their escape. I also didn't want the large, rowdy pit bulls living across the street popping by uninvited, off leash, for obvious reasons.

I hired a local handyman referred by a friend, and he hand-built us a beautiful fence. It took a few weeks since not everything you need to build anything on an island is readily available at Home Depot, nor can everything be shipped in a timely fashion. It took patience and a willingness to adjust and adapt, but eventually the fence was in place and mission accomplished, or so I thought.

One morning, while running errands upcountry about 30 minutes away from home, I got a call from a neighbor that Mikey was in his backyard. What?! While I was grateful for the call, I was puzzled how this 12-pound pup had possibly escaped. The thought of anything happening to this dog had me in tears.

I raced home, heart pounding, and picked up Mikey at my neighbor's house. He was covered in dirt which added to the "how did he get out" mystery. I thanked the neighbors for keeping him safe until I arrived. When I got to my house I realized what had happened. He'd dug a hole underneath the front gate to the fence, and wandered next door. This wasn't acceptable, and needed an immediate fix. The guy who built the fence came racing back over to discuss ideas on how to prevent Mikey from visiting the neighbors uninvited again in the future. Pouring a bit of concrete to prevent the possibility of a dog digging his way out was the easy solution. There was nothing wrong with the fence, in fact, it was one of the nicest, most solid fences I'd seen on the island. We'd just overlooked the fact that dogs can and will dig their way out if they think there's something happening on the other side of the fence.

Unfortunately, while fences (and concrete) can keep the pups secure, what can't be controlled are the actual neighbors and their poor behavior that get overlooked by local police who chalk it up to "island living." It's bound to happen living on an island—loud teens on motor bikes, people letting their large dogs run off-leash in the streets, late-night parties. Trying to have a conversation with stoned surfer neighbors is like trying to make sense to a newborn who has no idea what you're talking about.

Eventually, you either accept the island way of life, or you move out and try to find a quieter spot. I did the latter so that I could enjoy a bit more peace to read, write, work, meditate and also so that I could worry less about my pups' safety. The house I moved into was basically an enclosed compound, which we further reinforced with large river rocks (lots of them!) to block off any potential fencing gaps, and chicken wire-lined much of the fence for extra security. What I realized that I loved most about this particular house—apart from its proximity to the ocean and the adorable town of Pa'ia—were my neighbors. The front door to the house fronted an ancient Japanese cemetery, which meant zero noise (obviously I'm not kidding). And, right next door to the cemetery was a fenced-in, grassy pasture filled with goats of all sizes. This cracked me up when I first noticed them, but I then quickly felt drawn to say hello each time we walked by. My dogs became obsessed, literally, with the kids and it was the sweetest change of vibe from what we'd previously endured just five minutes down the road.

Switching up the home scene was a necessary move to get my peace and joy restored and it just wasn't possible, even on beautiful Maui, to live in peace when the neighbors were oblivious to anyone not on their late-night noisy agenda. The big lesson I learned on Maui with regards to neighbors is that you can't choose them, but you can choose how you react to them. Since I didn't want to tolerate sleepless nights and off-leash dogs in my driveway, I opted out of my lease at the end of it and found a much more peaceful spot nearby and even closer to the ocean that better suited my needs.

When I relocated to San Diego, I took a bit of a leap of faith and moved into a townhouse that friends had seen and FaceTimed me from. Initially, it seemed perfect as it was in a great location, at the right price and was only a few years old so everything appeared shiny and new. It opened up to a peaceful fountain in the courtyard and the décor had a sleek Zen vibe. What I've come to quickly realize is that you can't build a fence to shut out the neighbors when you share townhouse walls. If you only have one main window in your living room and it faces the shared courtyard, then you really can't open the blinds unless you enjoy living in a fishbowl. Living in a townhouse also isn't the greatest idea with multiple dogs. Neighbors are constantly opening and closing doors, chatting loudly in the courtyard and having workmen over to do all kinds of loud disruptive construction and home-fixes. It's anything but peaceful. While I can't build a fence or move to a goat pasture in my current setting, I did block the cell number of the very annoying neighbor who kept texting and calling me to ask questions about my unit and complain about my dogs. This sufficed in protecting my peace until I realized I needed a much bigger change.

And, as a complete plot twist to my life, I started thinking maybe it was time to buy a house and put down roots in a setting that DID feel the most peaceful and where I could feel at home. I started the search for a home along the coast, and within a few weeks had found the perfect house to buy as the owners had just completed a total renovation—in the same Zen, peaceful style that I would have chosen from top to bottom. I stopped worrying how I could make it happen, and I just made it happen. I stayed the course of trusting the universe and having faith bigger than my fear, even when an obnoxious mortgage broker tried to botch the deal when I didn't want to date him. I had to move money from my IRA to the escrow account to close the transaction—and there were a few hiccups that might have given others pause—but I knew deep down this was meant to be my house. It was the right move, that I have no doubt. I love the neighborhood, there is a gate to keep out those who do not live here, and my neighbors are friendly and kind. Everyone has dogs, and no one lets them run around off-leash. It works well for us, and the fenced-in back patio was definitely a selling point when I was deciding to buy the house. Fences always help, and I was thrilled not to have to build another one from scratch after the Maui experience. This place is already a "no pups escaping" zone. It's perfect. Fences make great neighbors. And, boundaries are something never to leave home without.

Neighbors Playlist/Lesson 7 Songs:

1:   White Fences, by NEEDTOBREATHE
2:   No Boundaries, by Kris Allen
3:   Peace and Quiet, by The I.L.Y's
4:   Happy, by Emma Stevens
5:   Bringing it Home, by Barenaked Ladies
6:   Gypsy, by Lady Gaga
7:   There Goes the Neighborhood, by Sheryl Crow
8:   Take Me Home, Country Roads, by John Denver
9:   My House, by Flo Rida
10: Work From Home, by Fifth Harmony

LESSON 8

Island Time is the Right Time, Trust the (Slow) Process

It didn't take me long living on Maui to learn the definition of "island time." It struck me early on when I saw a bumper sticker on the car in front of me that said: "Slow down, this isn't the mainland." Right. This wasn't an easy adjustment since I've always been that girl who shows up to an appointment at least 15 minutes early and to the airport hours in advance of my flight. I just always hated waiting for people, and I never wanted to be that person making someone else wait on my behalf. It was engrained in me at an early age that it's rude to be late, and disrespectful of others' time, so for decades I never showed up to a meeting even five seconds late. That is, until I moved to Maui and realized that no one pays much attention to the reality of time, everyone truly adheres to a theory of "island time" and you really don't have a choice but to slow down and adapt to the much slower locals' pace.

The sea turtles (honu) that hang out on the north shore at Baldwin Beach (where I'd typically start my Maui days with a peaceful meditative beach walk) were a constant reminder that slow progress is still progress. I was reminded daily that this is what I came to Maui for—a slower, easier pace of life as mine had been spinning out of control at warp speed for years. I even got a honu tattooed on my ankle, complete with a peace sign inside a heart on his shell, as a permanent note-to-self that it's more than okay to go slow.

Don't stop, just slow down, and know that there is no reason to race anywhere just to arrive early as most likely, no one else will be there on time. That's just how it goes on an island like Maui, and it's been a wonderful lesson in the art of slowing down and appreciating the present moment rather than worrying about what's ahead once I arrive wherever I am going.

When I originally set out to write this book, my working title was *Island Time*. I chose that as the original title because it summed up a few things for me, about me and my "on island" experiences that I wanted to share with the world. While others questioned my unconventional choices (including moving to Maui), I didn't really care. I needed a drastic change and I opted out of my glitzy busy LA life and took up residence on my favorite island by choice, and simply because it was time. My health was declining, my stress level was out of control, I wasn't feeling joyful despite the growing success of my business, and the grief and overwhelm from losing both parents had left me feeling foggy and unclear about my future goals. What I was very clear about however, was how much happier and more peaceful I felt each time I'd land on Maui for a visit, and after attending that weeklong retreat with Deepak and Mallika Chopra I had less-than-zero doubts that it was time for an extended dose of island time.

Moving away from the crazy busy pace of everyday life on the mainland was the obvious answer for me at a time when I honestly didn't know what I wanted my future to look like. I only knew that I had a better shot of figuring it out (and getting healthier) while living on island time. During my months on Maui, I developed a very strong understanding of what island time truly means.

Apart from the small collection of business people tied to constraints of off-island time-zone expectations, no one is ever in a hurry on Maui. There are schedules and shop hours that really only serve as guidelines; it's not unusual to arrive at a shop and find the "be back soon" sign in the window. It is what it is. It's Maui and if you're one of those workaholic, perfectionist, type-A+ people like me, you have two choices: 1) Get with the (much slower) program, or, 2) Leave.

It's unrealistic to expect anyone else to speed up; It's not in their nature, and they're on pace with the local culture and the prevailing "this isn't the mainland" attitude. I recall standing in line at the local market days after landing on the island tapping my foot subconsciously but clearly impatiently. The cashier told me that I should try to relax into the local vibe because she's the only one there to help customers and it's always going to take her a bit of time to get to me. I got the message loud and clear (Do not to come back with the same attitude I walked in with, and to bring my patience anywhere I went on the island). Roger that.

While at the time, I wanted the line to move faster and to get out of there and home to walk my pups, I never forgot the underlying tone of kindness from that cashier. She truly just wanted to infuse me with the reality of what I'd walked in to. I was the newcomer, the non-local, the jetsetter from Los Angeles who'd chosen Maui as my new home base. If I wanted the locals to embrace me, and be kind to me, I was going to have to do the same... and quickly, as island time is the only time that exists on Maui.

One of the coolest things about living on island time on Maui is that people tend to make the most of the daylight hours, and it was a reminder to do so no matter where in the world I am (when possible). On Maui, most rise early—literally with the crowing chickens. People head to the beach to ride waves or run or to do whatever brings them peace. Typically after the sun sets, the day is over and there's not a lot of late-night action. This schedule and way of life suited me perfectly. After years of being stretched way too thin, with not enough hours to rest in between morning meetings and late-night business dinners, I soon realized that I loved the mellowness of life on Maui.

The slow pace of the days that sometimes led to early bedtimes and a cycle of "early to bed, early to rise" was a departure from decades of being permanently jet-lagged and sleep deprived. It was foreign to me to feel well-rested, but my health improved immensely after months of catching up on sleep. I also recall what Deepak said at the Maui-based Living with Intention retreat about sleep having more to do with good health than nearly anything else. I took this to heart and put rest and sleep atop my priority list and continue to do so, even though I'm no longer physically on island time. It's just not possible to be productive and run a business with the necessary focus and clarity when you're exhausted. Try meditating when you're operating at 1000 mph daily. Ha. That's a joke. (I tried it... and eventually realized it only works when you are willing to breathe and slow down).

Slowing down the dial on pretty much everything has been essential for me back on the mainland, where I'm now consciously choosing to operate on a much lower speed than in my pre-Maui days. This doesn't mean at all that I'm not busy or not productive; quite the contrary. Knowing what to say no to and not overscheduling myself is a daily practice and a survival tactic for empaths like me according to Dr. Judith Orloff in her book *The Empath's Survival Guide.*

I only accept invites to business-related events and social gatherings that I'm genuinely excited about. If I feel any sort of angst when I review my calendar, I catch myself and realize I'm getting caught up in my old habits of trying to do too much and I edit out the non-essentials. Living on island time taught me that it's actually more than okay to have time to meditate, do yoga, chill with my dogs, go on beach walks, nap and sleep for a full eight hours a night. I LOVE this new speed of my life and try to stick with it, but some days it's simply impossible given the growth of my company, the move to a new house, the needs of three pups and the desire to have some semblance of a social life. But, at the end of the day, I know when I've got too much on my plate and I know when to say no and give my body and mind and soul time to recharge and catch up.

To be honest, there were days on Maui when I wanted things to speed up and I wanted to be doing anything but living life on island time. It isn't always in my nature to enjoy standing patiently in line at the store, listening to the cashier chat up local surfers. There were days I really did NOT have the patience to sit in my car on the one-way highway into my small north shore town that clogged up with tourists. Some days I didn't want to wait 15 minutes for my almond-milk latte; I came from LA where the baristas work at warp speed even at the busiest Starbucks in town.

Eventually, I surrendered. I gave in to the fact that it was my choice to live in a place where most people do not wear watches or pay attention to the time unless they have a flight to catch (and even then, many cut it quite close!). I learned that no one really ever texts or calls to tell you if they are running late, it's often just understood that time is just a guideline. I had a friend who liked to host people for lunch in his beautiful backyard, but after a few experiences of "lunch" being pushed to dinner after hours of swimming and sunning, I made sure to always eat something at home before I headed over there since it could be much later before the BBQ even got fired up.

Apart from the occasional frustrations that come when you're a recovering workaholic who is being pushed to slow down, learn patience and go with the flow, I found myself following the lead of the honu who crawl their way in and out of the sea with ease and slow grace. I tell myself on my busiest days: "Breathe. Slow progress is still progress." I cannot imagine going back to my previous way of "being" when I always had a to-do list a mile long, felt there weren't enough hours in the day, and had no idea how I'd get everything done.

Another takeaway from spending so much time on island time is that not everything is high-priority or needs immediate attention. Since that's an impossibility on an island like Maui, I learned to focus on what matters most. Some days, it has nothing to do with work or grown-up responsibilities, but it's about my mental, physical and emotional health which cannot operate at optimal levels if I'm burnt out from running around and spinning too hard and fast.

As the owner of a travel business, it's not lost on me that it's actually my job to encourage people to take breaks, as it's been proven to be beneficial to our health to disconnect, slow down, recharge and reconnect. I had to do all of this to truly absorb the benefits of life on island time. Not to sell anyone on the idea of taking a nice long vacation to Maui (or any other island that operates on a dialed-down pace), but it is a guaranteed prescription for a dose of peace and joy not easily found in "faster" spots and busy cities. And, no doctor's note required. Just a flight.

Tips for Living on Island Time a.k.a. "5 Ways to Slow the F*CK Down"

1: Take a full day off from work/family/the world, regardless of where you live, and put your phone/social media devices away. I used to think this was impossible, but the world can live without any of us for a day, trust me.

2: Spend time at the beach, or a nearby park. Just walking barefoot on the sand or in the grass for 15 minutes is meditative and will allow you to step away from distractions.

3: Stay off freeways for a week. Build in enough time to take the slower, more scenic route to wherever you are going.

4: Look at your calendar and cancel three things you aren't super excited about. No need to make excuses, just cancel in the name of putting your health and need for downtime ahead of everything else.

5: Meditate. Twice a day. Even if just for a few minutes a day, listen to a Deepak Chopra or Ask-Angels or Louise Hay (my favorite) meditation which you can find for free on YouTube. This should be non-negotiable time you give yourself daily.

Island Time Playlist/Lesson 8 Songs:

1: Catch my Breath, by Kelly Clarkson
2: Overwhelmed, by Rachel Platten
3: Power of Now, by Faith Rivera
4: I Allow, I Surrender, by Karen Drucker
5: I Remember Me, by Jennifer Hudson
6: Living in the Moment, by Jason Mraz
7: Take Your Sweet Time, by Jesse McCartney
8: On and On, by Michael Franti & Spearhead
9: Just Keep Breathing, by We The Kings

LESSON 9

No One Cares What You Do or What You Drive

"What do you want to be when you grow up?"

I'm pretty sure many of us heard this question at some point in our childhood and felt pressured to figure out the answer before we had a clue. It was a big question for a small child (I recall hearing it asked at a young age), yet this much I know: I never envisioned running a business selling luxury travel. Rather, I knew from a very young age that I wanted to be a writer and that my goal was to see my name in print in my favorite magazines. I went to college and got a magazine journalism degree. I did what I said I would do: I traveled around and wrote for magazines from age 21 through 35, when I somehow discovered that I had other things to do with my years of knowledge and expertise about global travel. I got a hit from above that I should be selling, not just writing about what I knew.

Selling luxury travel from my home office in South Florida back in 2005 was not exactly how I had envisioned the course of my career path, but that's where I found myself. And soon, I started answering the "What do you do?" question with a different answer than what had been the obvious answer for 15 years. Not being a journalist anymore left me to recreate and redefine my identity, as I could no longer answer the "What do you do?" question with the answer that defined me in my 20s and early 30s. It took years for me to ease into the comfort of saying "I sell luxury travel" rather than "I'm a journalist."

Once I ceased giving a shit if people judged me for being a "travel agent" based on their own pre-conceived notions, it took the pressure off of caring about others' perceptions. Eventually, I started to focus on building my high-level business, on my terms. I used social media and unconventional marketing tactics to generate revenue doing something I found I really enjoyed until the stress of the schedule and travel pushed me to do it differently, from a home on my favorite island in the middle of the ocean.

One of the absolute best things about living on an island like Maui is that you can truly do whatever you want for a living and no one judges, or for that matter, even cares. Quite the opposite, in fact. The entire time I was there, I think maybe only three people asked me what I did for a living. It was pretty refreshing not needing to explain that I sell luxury travel (and then have to answer the "Oh really, you're a travel agent?" follow-up question).

Occasionally, the topic of career choice would come up with friends who literally had no idea what I did when I wasn't playing tennis, walking my dogs or chasing rainbows and riding waves at the beach (as my Instagram feed might have led one to believe), and inevitably it would result in a surprised look and a response to the tune of "Really? You run a travel business?" For some reason, it sounded impossible to those who only knew me as the peaceful, beach-loving, flip-flop wearing yogi I'd morphed into on Maui, not the type-A workaholic I'd identified with in previous chapters of my life.

After decades of working like crazy to build a successful business and to become who I thought I needed and wanted to be (the jet-setting business owner wearing fancy clothes and attending events around the globe while juggling writing assignments and travel booking requests in all time zones), I found it peace-inducing to work quietly in the privacy of my home and not even discuss it with my Maui friends. It was a lot more fun to talk with my island friends about what time our tennis match was or which beach we would meet up at for lunch on Saturday. My time on Maui was not only a needed respite from the tiring schedule that had put my physical and mental health in jeopardy, but it was a big fat break from feeling the need to answer that basic but burning question I'd been asked for decades: "What do you do?"

For so many years, this was the question that couldn't be avoided. People naturally want to ask and know the answer to what it is we "DO." What I learned on Maui was that people couldn't care less how you make your money. Whether you clean houses, teach surfing or send clients on expensive vacations, your job does not define who you are. People want to know what you like to do in your spare time and they don't question how you earn the funds to live in a nice house or drive a nice car. And, if you do drive a nice car, you quickly learn that it's kind of silly to do so as the island air and ocean salt and winds take its toll. Couple that with spending a lot of time at the beach and finding your car endlessly filled with sandy towels, wet dogs and athletic bags filled with clothes from your daily activities. It explains why even the wealthiest people on Maui typically drive older SUVs, open-air Jeeps and small, fuel-efficient cars that can easily be parked on the side of roads when space is at a premium.

No one cares what you drive because it doesn't define who you are. As someone who's a bit OCD about keeping my car super-clean and neat, I had to surrender to the reality of how impossible this was. I'd shipped over my nice new Lexus SUV in 2016 and within a few months, I no longer enjoyed driving it because it smelled like mildew and surf. No matter what I tried, it wasn't possible to keep a nice car clean and nice. It got to the point that I wanted to drive a Maui "Cruiser" like many of my friends did. Stuck in year two of a three-year lease, I told myself I'd give back the Lexus as soon as possible and buy a decent but not-too-nice Jeep better suited for island life if I opted to make Maui my long-term home (something that was still up for consideration).

Driving around the island as I often did for fun—with sandy feet from impromptu pull-overs at the beach for a quick meditation, swim, walk, or all three—my car was destined for consistent messiness. There is also a shortage of car washes on Maui, so finding time to clean the car was something I just couldn't get caught up in. I slowly gave into the need to just surrender and embrace the "no one cares what you drive" mentality. Years of working hard to be able to afford leases on "nice" cars ranging from BMWs to Lexus convertibles and SUVs were totally unimportant in this new phase of my life. I honestly don't think anyone ever paid attention to what kind of car I got into at the valet station at my favorite restaurant Mama's Fish House. They only cared that you move quickly out of the way so the next white Jeep (the tourist favorite) could pass by.

Funny enough, when I decided to move back to the mainland, the Lexus I formerly loved started to fail me. The left door handle suddenly stopped working a day before the car was due to ship to San Diego. The smell of the surf and wet towels couldn't be erased, despite multiple detail attempts. The air-conditioning started making noise. I felt like my car was trying to tell me something, as my overworked and tired body had when I first got to Maui. Enough was enough. It was time to put this "too nice for island life" car to rest.

When I returned to California, I picked up my messy Lexus SUV at the Port of San Diego and immediately felt like it was time to make a change. I didn't enjoy driving the car with the surf racks I'd installed at the request of my former fiancé (who taught surfing for a living). I had time left on the lease and was unsure if I had any options other than waiting it out until the lease ended. I found myself thinking about looking into possibilities as soon as I got settled in San Diego, but it wasn't top priority. Then, at the end of a blind date, the guy—who I had been hesitant to meet—told me he was driving me home in a crappy rental car because his Porsche Cayenne was in the shop. For some reason, I knew he was lying (the red flags couldn't be ignored) but the conversation triggered my own inner-Porsche fantasy and next thing I knew, I found myself test-driving my own version of my dream car: a black-on-black Porsche Cayenne. This car symbolized a lot about where I currently was in my life after coming full circle back to the mainland motivated to reboot my business and passions.

I wasn't going to say yes to the Porsche to prove anything to anyone else. This wasn't anyone else's dream car, it was wholly mine. Without even thinking twice, I said yes to the sales girl, wrote a check and signed the paperwork. I also felt my dad's presence there in the showroom with me. I heard him from above saying: "Get the Porsche, and get it in black." My dad was always a fan of fancy cars, and was the cool dad who had the 280Z with T-tops while I was in high school. This Porsche wasn't only my dream car, but it was his too. Whenever I drive it, it makes me smile because it feels safe and fun and fast and illustrates what I was afraid of for years: Committing to something that is a bit out of my comfort zone. I've finally gotten to the point however, where I don't let old limiting beliefs steal my joy.

These days, I take what I learned on Maui and put it to daily use in how I run my business and my life. I am thrilled to answer the question of what I do when new neighbors, who are genuinely interested in knowing more about me, inquire at a dinner party. No one is judging me for choosing "luxury travel" as a career path. The reaction is more one of "Oh, really, you've traveled the world? Where have you been? Maybe you can help us plan a future travel experience."

By surrounding myself with like-minded interesting entrepreneurial types I've found it enjoyable once again to discuss what I do for a living. That said, I never forget what Deepak said that day at the Maui retreat that changed my life: *"You don't need to quit your day job to be who you truly are. What you do for a living doesn't define who you are and it's more than okay to keep the day job that allows you to live in abundance and share your gifts with others."*

Not a day goes by that I don't feel grateful for having found a way to make a living in a way that allows me to not only enjoy my life but to change others' lives for the better by facilitating incredible experiences for them. I enjoy being a first-world problem solver, I love being compensated for bringing joy to my clients in the form of priceless memories gained via traveling the world in style.

I also love driving my Porsche. And, that's okay. It's more than okay to love your life, and to love what you do and what you drive, because it's still essential to slow down and pay attention to the rules of the road as they apply to daily life. I was reminded recently when I got into a fender bender of my own fault that even Porsches are still prone to popping tires if you don't take roundabouts and "caution, go slow" signs carefully.

I had flashbacks to past experiences as I sat there waiting for the Porsche roadside assistance guy to come with a tow and the dealer to send the driver with a loaner. I felt extra-thankful that only my tires, not me or the pups or anyone else, were damaged when I swerved and hit the curb of the new-to-me roundabout in my new San Diego neighborhood. Before panicking (as I would have done in my pre-Maui days), I texted my new neighbor who showed up five minutes later to pick up the pups who were in the car with me when it happened (the day before Thanksgiving!). Because I stayed calm and didn't freak out, and because I looked up and said, "Thank you God, thank you for the reminder that a car can be replaced and that if money ($600) can fix the problem (tires) it's not a real problem." I got an instant message from above that Porsches, like people, are not invincible. Both can be damaged, and both can be repaired. My first car was a tiny red Mitsubishi Mirage. I never felt safe driving it, and it's probably because I got into a terrible accident on the highway driving from Washington, DC to meet my family in upstate NY. Those memories stuck with me for years. While I obviously survived the accident, the car was a totaled mess.

I've always valued the feeling of safety and security and that's still highly important to me. It's probably why driving a Porsche Cayenne feels right to me, because it's a symbol of how hard I've worked to get to a place where I have the freedom to choose the car I want to drive. It's not about what anyone else thinks. It's all about finding what brings me joy and comfort in my own space. That's what it can be about for anyone who's serious about letting go of outside perceptions, dropping all judgments (of self and others) and truly not caring what anyone does or drives. NO ONE CARES ☺ so JUST DO YOU.

No One Cares Playlist/Lesson 9 Songs:

1: Just Do You, by India.Arie
2: Drive, by Ben Rector

3: Good To Be Alive, by Jason Gray
4: Drive By, by Train
5: Do What U Want, Lady Gaga
6: Fast Car, by Tracy Chapman
7: Hey Porsche, by Nelly
8: Double Life, by The Cars

LESSON 10

Choosing JOY is
Always an Option

If I can do it, anyone can. No, really. That's my story and I am sticking to it. I've been to hell and back and hit rock bottom on the grief and trauma and fear and anger and unhappiness trains enough times now to know that there is ALWAYS an option to get off that train and consciously CHOOSE JOY.

As Deepak Chopra, Marianne Williamson, Wayne Dyer, Louise Hay, Yogi Bhajan, Gabrielle Bernstein, Nancy Levin, Christiane Northrup, Judith Orloff and the other spiritual teachers and authors who have impacted me the most like to say: "Happiness is Your Birthright."

No matter what happens TO you, it's actually happening FOR you. The only way to heal the pain is to feel the pain, and then release it. Forgive everyone for everything. Let that shit go. Ha, I've heard it all. I've meditated on it for years now. Years of living in the darkness came to a screeching halt the day my mom died. That's the day I cracked open and knew that I no longer had a choice to pretend that everything was okay. NOTHING was okay. I was an orphan and I had no freaking clue what was coming next. I knew that JOY was the opposite of how I felt that day, and for days and months to follow. But, I also made the conscious choice to heal differently than I had when my dad died. That took me years to recover from, and it required the help of mind-numbing antidepressants that didn't get to the root of the grief but it did soften the initial blow. When my mom died at 67, my heart shattered. I was broken, all over. I had to heal a lot deeper this time.

The awakening that happened to me and through me and continues to shake me on a daily basis has led me to an incredibly different perspective on how life is meant to be lived. Once I did the work to get past the initial phases of shock and grief, and worked with my therapist (using various forms of EMDR, tapping, hypnosis, and energy release) to process the guilt and anger and fear and everything else that steamrolls through you when your mom dies, I was able to breathe more peacefully than in decades. I realized that it was completely my choice how I was going to move forward from here. Was I going to wallow in grief and anger and misery over losing both parents to cancer way too young? Was I going to allow my business to suffer because my physical and mental and emotional health weren't firing on all levels? Was I going to ruin relationships with people who tried to get close to me at a time when I just couldn't possibly explain why I was such a mess? I didn't have the answers at the time the world felt like it was crushing me, but I did know I had choices.

The first major choice I made was to stick with a non-negotiable commitment to a year of intense therapy to face head-on everything I'd danced around for decades. As the "strong" one in the family and the CEO of my company, no one—including me—really knew the real me. The only way this journey to joy was going to be successful was if I stopped pretending that I had a clue how life was supposed to go. I knew nothing other than I didn't want to be sad and mad and guilt-ridden for the rest of my life. I felt numb but I also knew, as my grandma always told me, "This too shall pass."

One of the first steps in liberating yourself and allowing yourself to choose joy is to accept that whatever shit you are going through, and no matter how much it hurts, it's always temporary. Healing isn't linear. There is no timeline for how long it will take until you stop feeling sad and mad and grief-ridden. Hell, I still have those days when I just want to stay in bed and cry because I'm PMS'ing on top of it being an "I miss my mom/dad/grandma/ex-boyfriend" kind of day. Those days, however, happen less frequently, because I automatically turn to my self-care toolkit (see next lesson for more on this) and rely on the techniques I know are tried and true.

Whether it's lighting peppermint candles and lying in bed with my three dogs while listening to an uplifting meditation or audiobook on positive thinking, joy, self-healing, angels, self-love; booking a deep-tissue massage, acupuncture, reiki or infrared sauna session to move out some of the stuck sad energy; head to the beach for a long meditative walk; call an inner-circle friend who gets me; putting down work for the day and just going to a yoga class or some other form of energy movement, I know what I need to do to realign my chakras, release some (if not all) of the stuck energy and call on my healers, wellness practitioners and guides to support me on my path to choosing joy.

I am the first to admit that some days are harder than others. We live in a world where there is so much nonsense happening that people who've not experienced real trauma mistake it for important. People DO sweat the small stuff. People DO get annoyed over such unimportant crap. None of us are immune from getting annoyed over shit that truly doesn't matter; what's essential is how we recognize and recover from it. What good does it do our own soul to get annoyed at the friend who canceled dinner plans because she drank too much the previous night and is home sick unable to get out of bed? Yep, true story. This bugged me when I got a text at 3 p.m. from my hungover friend, until a minute later I thought to myself, "I didn't really want to go out tonight anyway. She just gave me an easy out." The next time I saw her, she apologized and I hugged her and our friendship remains strong because we both know how to let shit go that isn't worth holding onto.

I find that by letting people be who they are, learn their own lessons, and make their own choices, it's freed me up to do the same. As a textbook Scorpio, I've never liked being told what to do, when to do it, how to do it. In fact, anyone who tells me how to do something is probably not going to see that happen. It's in my nature to go with my gut, follow my intuition, listen to my guides, and do what I instinctively know is best. That said, others do not always see it this way and may think I'm rebellious or defiant. As a child, that's what I recall taking away as the message. As an adult, I now see that I can much more easily be peaceful and joy-filled when I don't give in to doing anything in any way that doesn't feel good or right to me.

I don't go to events or parties or business functions out of obligation, the way I did for years. I simply can't justify saying yes to doing anything, going anywhere, or spending time with anyone that doesn't add joy to my life. I've been using this as my "party line" now for a few years. Traveling nonstop for decades to attend conferences in countries around the world appeared fun and glamorous but it was killing me, literally, as a mono/anemia/toxic mercury diagnosis made that clear.

When I finally put the kibosh on the excessive traveling and turned the focus to grounding myself so that I could get healthy, the fog began to lift. I felt my entire being light up when I made the intuitive decision to follow my heart and soul to Maui in April 2016. The time I spent on the island in the middle of the ocean (which used to terrify me but now soothes my soul) was all part of the larger plan. I get it now. I have a much bigger purpose on this planet than I could have possibly known before losing both parents and experiencing the horrendous level of pain that accompanies life-altering losses. That's the silver lining, I guess.

The peace I've been able to find after deciding it's what was most important to me is something I would not trade for anything. Even when I was challenged in the midst of the break-up with the totally wrong guy I almost married on Maui, my coach asked me: "What is most important to you?" She knew I was upset at the amount of money I had thrown away on a car, new clothes, travel and all kinds of things for this guy, yet she also knew I had a successful business and could fortunately generate revenue to quickly replace what I'd wasted on him. My answer to her question came out of my mouth as if on auto-play: "Peace and joy." To which she replied, "Not money?" No, I told her, there is not enough money in the world to replace what it feels like to have peace and joy. I came to Maui to find peace and experience joy, and that's the train I got back on—and have stayed on since. Just because I took a little detour and got engaged, and then broke up with a guy who wasn't for me, didn't mean that was going to derail my newly-found focus on what is most important as I uncover my true passions and purpose in this lifetime.

The healers/wellness friends I made on the island and in Los Angeles and now in San Diego over the past few years are those I credit with helping me see how detrimental it was to be carrying around decades of built-up resentment, anger, guilt, sadness, fear and grief. It is a LOT to walk through in life. Only when I truly committed to a daily practice of grief release, energy clearing and acts of joy (literally, figuring out what brings me joy and making sure that's on my daily to-do list) was I able to confidently walk the walk, talk the talk. You cannot inspire others to work through their own crap and come out on the other side as a joy chooser if you aren't doing it yourself.

The bottom line: Everyone goes through shit in their lives. It's how you consciously decide to work through it that is ultimately going to determine if you let it piss you off long enough to steal your joy, or if you value peace and joy enough to stay the course. Once you realize how much happier you are when you opt to choose joy, it's pretty impossible to do anything else. Choose joy, no matter how crappy life seems. There is always someone going through something worse than you are, and you are always strong enough to handle whatever happens as part of your life plan.

Asking for help from above, trusting that the universe has your back (as another favorite author Gabrielle Bernstein always says), and always letting your faith be bigger than your fear is what will get you through those darker days. That, and a spiritual self-care toolkit (to be revealed in Lesson 11!).

My short list of joy-raising tips:

1. Listen to music you love
2. Play with puppies (yours or others)
3. Take a walk by the beach, feel sunshine on your face
4. Call (don't text) a favorite inner-circle friend
5. Get reiki, cranio sacral or energy-releasing massage
6. Stay away from negative people who steal your joy
7. Take the day off from work (clients will understand)
8. Listen to anything by Louise Hay or Wayne Dyer
9. Cancel any plans that don't excite you
10. Say yes to whatever DOES bring you joy

Choose Joy Playlist/Lesson 10 Songs:

1: Happy, by Pharrell Williams
2: Beautiful, by Carole King
3: Lookin' Up, by Barenaked Ladies
4: I Make My Own Sunshine, by Alyssa Bonagura
5: Dancing, by Kylie Minogue
6: Party in the U.S.A., by Miley Cyrus
7: Everybody Just Wants To Dance, by Kris Allen
8: 11:59, by Michael Franti & Spearhead
9: Stacy's Mom, by Fountains of Wayne
10: You Could Be Happy, by Snow Patrol

LESSON 11

Health is True Wealth and Self-Care is NOT Selfish

Self-care—the wellness buzzword of the decade—isn't something I knew until recently (after my year on Maui) is not only acceptable but necessary. I had to learn these lessons for my own sake on my own, as an adult in my 40s. I didn't grow up in a family where being selfish was a good thing, rather, it simply meant you cared less about others than yourself. After a year on an island where people really do prioritize their own health and happiness, I learned that it's more than okay to take care of yourself in a way that allows you to then be there in a better and healthier way for others. In other words, that old saying that you really do need to put your own oxygen mask on first is a million percent true. You can't save anyone if you don't save yourself.

No one talked about any of this while I was growing up, nor was it discussed in high school or college. In my 20s and 30s, when I was running around the world and operating on auto-pilot, I had no clue what the late nights, lack of sleep, and serious stress of building a new business was doing to my body, mind and soul. I didn't know anything was wrong because I looked fine, most of the time.

As author and self-care proponent Glennon Doyle posted recently on Instagram: "People who need help sometimes don't look like people who need help." That summed up exactly who I was for too many years. I knew what I needed to do to look the part of the successful, well-dressed, healthy and fit jet-setting CEO. But inside, I was exhausted, stressed out, and in all honestly, crumbling. Fancy clothes, perfect blow-outs and trendy Jimmy Choos can't hide the pain when serious illnesses like mono and anemia and trauma and stress are brewing. Add in a few traumatic losses and it gets harder to hide the angst, but it's still possible because it feels taboo to look the part of the broken soul (especially when you've always been the strong one!). No one really wants to hear how crappy you are feeling; they just want you to be that strong friend (colleague, girlfriend, sister) they've always perceived you to be.

For many years, prior to ditching my LA life and heading to Maui, my identity was defined by my "glamorous" job as a jet-setting journalist and then as a business owner who changed others' lives via travel experiences. Traveling all over the globe, visiting hotels, dining at fancy restaurants with company founders and scouting hot new locations is what I did practically on auto-pilot. I would do my best to "eat healthy" and try to recharge in between trips, but it was pretty hopeless. I didn't know the meaning of (or the need for) integrative health or functional medicine. No one was really yet talking "vitamin shots," mercury detox, energy healing, reiki or kundalini yoga. These incredible healing modalities hadn't yet presented themselves to me as ways I could be boosting my immune system, strengthening my soul, or repairing a damaged digestion system. I was a mess and I felt like hell.

After my mom died, I was barely sleeping. My irregular sleep patterns were constantly challenged by jetlag, back pain, headaches, memory fogginess, and overall fatigue that never seemed to go away for good. My doctor in Los Angeles prescribed weekly vitamin IV drips (ouch!), more red meat (to boost my scarily low iron), and told me to drink lots of orange juice (to pump up my vitamin C). She also said rest would help. I thought I had life under control, but life had me fooled.

A few weeks before my annual Maui year-end holiday in 2014, I was in London scouting new hotels before heading off to an annual luxury travel conference in the south of France. It should have been a blast! But, I literally felt worse than I ever remember feeling which made this trip anything but a plum assignment. I recall needing to sit down on the freezing cold steps of the Tube after a quick ride across the city because I thought I was going to pass out. My traveling companion didn't know what to make of my "sudden" serious illness, and honestly, it was puzzling to me too. I had the worst headache and my throat felt raw. It came on so suddenly and wouldn't let up the rest of my trip. I had to fake-smile my way through the conference with thousands of industry colleagues, while politely declining dinner invites and instead going to sleep as soon as the meetings ended each day. I was NOT myself and it was scary being in France feeling this way.

I flew home doped up on cold meds and saw my doctor immediately. She sent me for bloodwork as she suspected I had mono, and said it had probably been a low-grade virus in my system as Epstein-Barr for years. So basically, I'd been feeling like shit for years and had no idea this was why. As crazy as it sounded to be diagnosed with mono in my mid-40s, I was actually grateful when she called (the day I landed on Maui for a two-week stay) with the news that her hunch was correct. She told me to rest as much as possible, to NOT exercise or play tennis daily as

I had planned, to eat lots of iron and drink lots of vitamin C, and to come see her the day I got back to discuss further treatment strategies.

This was the start of my full-blown journey into my own #HealthIsWealth campaign, and my decision to make self-care and healing my top priority. Everything else seemed less important once I realized how sick I'd been for years. The stress of caring for sick parents, the reality of watching them both die, the aftermath of being an orphan, the stress of running a global growing business with high-powered clients counting on me to be on my A-game, and the daily demands of life finally knocked me down. It's exactly what I needed, that mono diagnosis. It led me to switching doctors in Los Angeles to one who specialized in auto-immune diseases and a more holistic approach to wellness. She quickly determined that eliminating toxic mercury and heavy metals present in my system was my most-pressing health concern. If we didn't address these issues, the physical pain, mental fog, fatigue, and inability to manage stress would continue to worsen.

If you glance at the Instagram pages of anyone in the health and spiritual healing worlds, the unmissable buzzword of those of us on a path to optimal wellness is "SELF-CARE." As in: Self-care is a necessity and it's definitely NOT selfish to put your own health and well-being on the short list of priorities. Gone are the days when taking care of yourself was seen as unimportant, or worse, something to hide.

In my world, having learned the hard way by experiencing serious illness, I know the meaning of health is wealth. It's priceless to be healthy, on all levels. Think about it: What good is anything else if you wake up daily feeling like crap (and often not knowing why)? If you can't enjoy your life because you are mentally or physically drained, you aren't helping anyone if you forego self-care. No one else can "fix" your health, it's on you to navigate that self-care path. I definitely got that memo a few years ago.

Exhausted from life, it took a solid year of ditching judgment in favor of an immersion in self-care while on Maui. I put healing decades of health issues atop my priority list—above my business, friendships and relationships—and quickly discovered the positive effect on not just me but everyone in my life. Once my health improved, so did all of my relationships. Interesting how that works.

At some point, I stopped caring what other people thought of me and followed my inner-island-girl-guidance to Maui where no one cares what you do for a living. I LOVED being in a place where it's *de rigeur* to wear sundresses and flip-flops while driving around the island to reiki healers, rolfers, acupuncturists, energy workers, massage therapists, a life coach, my naturopath and anyone else I connected with and felt could help me on my healing journey. Self-care became my mantra, as I committed to a lifetime philosophy of "health is wealth." Losing my parents to cancer shook up any illusions I had about life being easy or fair—but in a good way—as it forced me to focus on following a different path, consciously focused on healing my own health issues before they escalated into life-threatening ones. No freaking way.

I wish I'd known years ago how helpful it would be to douse myself in self-care. I mean, I kind of knew, but I always felt like I had to stay quiet about my love for finding time to squeeze in a massage or opting out of scheduled activities to simply sit in my hotel room drinking tea, reading a book, and shutting out the outside world. I always felt like I had to do this type of stuff in private, as if I was doing something wrong by shielding myself from everyone wanting to talk to or text or email with me. Little did I know, I was guiding myself in the direction my soul was craving to go... down the path of self-care and optimal health, on all levels.

When I reflect on when exactly I realized the need to focus on my health, flashbacks of various incidents pop into my brain… almost like a movie of someone else's life. Except, it's really my own true story of getting honest and coming to terms with what was derailing my ability to function properly, on all levels, mentally, emotionally and physically. And, that wasn't an option. Getting better was my immediate goal, and being healthy was my long-term plan. The year on Maui taught me that focusing on self-care was a survival strategy, and it still is.

It's been a major work-in-progress and it continues. Since landing back on the mainland, I've focused on getting grounded and finding my village in San Diego. It definitely does take a village of like-minded, conscious self-care advocates who practice what they preach. My naturopath in San Diego lit up my life recently when she shared with me that my blood tests came back showing everything important in the "normal" range. A few years ago I heard the exact opposite—nothing was normal! Several years of consistent focus on tuning into my body, listening to the messages instead of ignoring them, paying attention to the need for less hard-core cardio workouts in favor of more time meditating and doing gentle yoga and taking beach walks is what got my heath back on track.

When my naturopath asked me what my picture of self-care looked like, it was a simple answer. Every day I listen to my body. I schedule something daily that is good for my mind, body and soul no matter how busy I may be. This could be a therapeutic massage, a physical therapy session, a visit to the chiropractor, a private Pilates class, a walk on the beach, an appointment with a medium, a reiki master or an energy worker. There are SO many things I enjoy including in my self-care regime because the positive "health report card" I received reflects the positive effects these stress-reducing modalities and treatments have on me. Never will I feel guilty spending money on or investing time in my health and wellness, as it truly is more important than everything else in life. It took a year on Maui immersed in island life to fully embrace and understand how okay it is to put your own health ahead of everything else. Just do it. HEALTH IS WEALTH.

Self-Care Tips for Your Own Spiritual Tool-Kit

1: Schedule a daily "good for me" appointment, whether it's a massage, a solo walk or an hour-long meditation.
2: Stop traveling more than you need to while focusing on improving your health. Stay grounded for a year.
3: Rescue a dog if you don't already have one; the love from a pup is a perfect Rx during your healing process.
4: Sleep when you are tired. Drink tons of water. Cut out sugar. Eat nourishing foods.
5: Learn to embrace the term #JOMO (Joy of Missing Out) as it means you are focused on your health and not compelled to be anywhere but in your healing environment.
6: Read a lot of books by Caroline Myss, Pema Chodron, Marianne Williamson, Nancy Levin, Louise Hay & Gabrielle Bernstein
7: Find a good naturopathic doctor in your area. Be open to alternative healing modalities.
8: Listen to your body. Rest. Recharge. That's not doing nothing; it's doing exactly what you need on your path to optimal health.

Self-Care Playlist/Lesson 11 Songs:

1: The Healing Song, by Karen Drucker
2: Chicken Soup in a Song, by India.Arie
3: This Is Me, by Kesha

4: Strong Enough, by Sheryl Crow

5: I Am Light, by India.Arie

6: The Climb, by Miley Cyrus

7: Live Like We're Dying, by Kris Allen

8: Forever Young, by Alphaville

LESSON 12

Live Pono, Have Hope, Keep the Faith and Practice Aloha

A year ago, I was on Maui reflecting on all I'd experienced living on island time, knowing intuitively that my time there was coming to a close. It was time to re-enter a different, happier version of life in California even though I didn't know exactly what it would look like. San Diego was calling to me. Los Angeles was a chapter ready to close. Maui will always be the place I remember as the magical island where I transformed into a better, softer, kinder version of myself. It's the place that allowed me to just be, not do. It's where I stopped running at a crazy pace and enjoyed sunrise beach walks and sunset viewings and rainbows, often. I stopped taking time for granted. I lived in a state of gratitude for all the natural beauty at every turn, and I got a crash course in the meaning of *living pono* (doing the right thing) and practicing aloha (spreading love and positivity everywhere). I didn't just practice the game of having hope and keeping the faith, I lived by it. I even got *hope&faith* tattooed on my arm as a reminder of what's most important, always.

Fast forward one year: I find myself writing the last chapter of this book about lessons an island taught me about "living my dreams" at the counter of my newly renovated kitchen in the dreamy San Diego beach house I bought and closed on last month. WHAT?! I know, I know. Homeowner status shocked me a bit too. I didn't quite see this plot twist coming. But, here I am, a homeowner in Carlsbad, California (the location where my serious spiritual journey started down the street at The Chopra Center in 2015). While none of it makes sense or is how I thought my story would flow, it all makes total sense when I think about all I've been putting into practice as a daily mantra on repeat: *Hope. Faith. Peace. Love. Do what you love. Live where you love. Live your dreams.*

Not long ago, I was bitching about an obnoxious landlord who was trying to kick out my third dog. I wasn't entirely feeling at home in the townhome I'd leased for the year sight unseen, as a way to get re-entered into mainland life. Instead of seeking out yet another rental that would force me to live by someone else's rules in someone else's property, I got online and started searching for better options. I connected with a realtor the next day and the house hunt began. Within a few weeks the perfect house in the perfect location with the perfectly just-finished remodel showed up and my offer was accepted.

I'm literally pinching myself while writing this last chapter about living pono, having hope, keeping the faith and practicing aloha—the biggest lessons I learned while on island time—from the dream house I miraculously bought all by myself last month. I say miraculously because truly, I had no idea my dream home was within reach. I had hope, I kept the faith. And, now I own the house I've always dreamed of living in thanks to all that time I spent on Maui meditating and being still and asking for answers from above about what I truly wanted for this next chapter of my life. I put in the work on the self-care/healing front. I learned the meaning of living pono and practicing aloha and I put them into practice daily, wherever I am.

While my travel business is successful and consistently growing, I'm a creative, big-picture entrepreneur and visionary. I am not the CFO/accountant type and to be honest, I had not focused on my finances enough to know that I could make my dream house a reality any time soon. I just kept the faith that it would work out if it was supposed to (the same way my move to Maui did!). I never lost hope in the turbulent mortgage process because I knew all was moving in the right direction, even on the days it felt a bit scary. I didn't let fear of not having enough money get in my way of searching out and quickly (within weeks) finding the perfect house. And most importantly, I didn't let a past experience owning a house in Florida that turned out to be a terrible investment stop me from forging ahead with buying my dream house in San Diego. I also didn't let anyone else's judgment or negative chatter cloud what I intuitively knew was the absolute right move for me, at the right time, even if it meant pouring everything I'd earned that year into the down payment. Literally.

A few months prior to sitting down to finish this book about what a year on Maui taught me about living my dreams, I had less-than-zero clue where I'd physically be writing it. But holy shit, I am a homeowner. I am writing the last chapter of this book in a house that I still cannot really believe is all mine. Well, I can believe it because my first mortgage payment came due and there were funds in my account to cover it. No one helped me get here financially. I do not have a trust fund, a wealthy family or a husband/partner in this venture. What I do have is endless amounts of faith and hope that the universe rewards risk takers, intuition followers and those brave enough to not back away from their true desires, especially when opportunities show up to make the big brave choice.

My life is my example of all of this. I'm just being me, following my heart and soul to where I feel most at peace and happiest. It has nothing to do with anyone else. I love the life I have created. I love myself for being resilient enough to get up and try again every time something didn't work out. I felt the pain. I acknowledged it. I went to Maui when I felt my life crumbling. I learned how to restore my health and wellness through a full-blown focus on healing old wounds, destroying less-than-useful limiting beliefs imprinted on me from early on, and most of all, by living by the Hawaiian philosophies of living pono and practicing aloha, always. I'm reminded daily that I am in the right place, right time. All that Maui taught me is coming full circle. Live pono. Practice aloha. Have hope. Keep the faith. Over and over and over. Do the right thing and you'll end up right where you are supposed to be.

I've been fortunate enough to travel the world a few times and unlike many of my friends, I do NOT have adventures like climbing Mount Kilimanjaro on my bucket list. Rather, buying this house has proven to be my version of Kilimanjaro; on a different scale, it was a serious uphill climb. But, having reached the summit, it's time to embrace what it feels like being settled and grounded. It's downhill from here. I've experienced more trauma and drama in this lifetime than many will ever know, and despite all of it, I am at the top of the mountain because I chose to climb it on my terms.

I am just relieved to be where I am, and for the first time in my life, I don't have a burning sense of wondering "What's NEXT?" I don't need to know what is next, because the happy ending to this book is that I am truly happy. It has nothing to do with anyone else. I don't yet have the love of my life manifested fully in my life, but I am confident he will show up soon...now that I've done the work, gotten healthy, cleared out lingering sadness, grief and darkness and replaced my cracked and broken heart with a new, clean, shiny healthy one ready to give and receive unconditional love—the type I currently get from my three rescue pups, Mikey, Romeo and of course, Pono.

A healer friend recently hugged me and told me: "Stacy, I am so happy for you. Look at where you are and how much work you've done to get here. For the first time in your life, it's obvious you now know the feeling of contentment." WOW. She is on point. I have had plenty of good experiences in my life, close encounters with love, but never truly have I had the level of unconditional love and pure, authentic happiness and joy that I now feel. As for what's next? That's up to the universe and I am open and ready to experience ALL of it. It does not matter what occurred in the past. That is OLD news. History. Nothing in the past can be redone differently. Forgiveness is key to moving forward, so forgive yourself for everything you might wish had not occurred. Whatever happened, happened. Whatever will be, will be. Just keep living pono, having hope, keeping the faith and practicing aloha. Don't be afraid to take risks, change your life and live your dreams. As I've said all along, WHY NOT ME?!? And more importantly, why not you?

Tips on Living Pono and Practicing Aloha

1. Just do the right thing. Always. If it doesn't feel right, don't do it.
2. Try saying "aloha" instead of hello to people, and watch them smile. Everyone reacts well to a dose of heartfelt Hawaiian-style aloha.
3. Know that it's better to be kind than right. This plays right into doing the right thing, always.
4. Adopt a senior rescue dog in need (this is definitely doing the right thing!).

5. Let someone go in front of you at the grocery store if you're not in a hurry. This will always make someone's day better.

6. Get thee to Maui. Spend a few days on this magical island and it's pretty impossible not to be swept up in the aloha spirit.

7. Spend time in meditation daily as it allows your mind to be still and your heart to clear. Only when you are still and clear, can you truly envision yourself living your absolute best life filled with high vibrations, positive energy and people who practice aloha and live pono.

Pono Aloha Hope and Faith Playlist/Lesson 12 Songs:

1: Pinch Me, by Barenaked Ladies
2: Riding Free, by Maisy Stella
3: Fearless, by Taylor Swift
4: Hope, by Jack Johnson
5: Keeping the Faith, by Billy Joel
6: Pono Aloha, by Hui Ohana
7: A Beautiful Day, by India.Arie
8: Today Is Beautiful, by David Dunn
9: First Day of My Life, by Bright Eyes
10: Do It For The Love, by Michael Franti & Spearhead

-THE END-

CPSIA information can be obtained
at www.ICGtesting.com
Printed in the USA
BVHW080753230220
573066BV00002B/253